Nicely Nurdled, Sir!

CHRISTOPHER LEE

Nicely Nurdled, Sir!

ELM TREE BOOKS · LONDON

First published in Great Britain 1986
by Elm Tree Books/Hamish Hamilton Ltd
27 Wrights Lane London W8 5TZ

British Library Cataloguing in Publication Data

Lee, C. R. A.
  Nicely nurdled sir!
  1. Cricket
  I. Title
  796.35'8   GV917
  ISBN 0-241-11402-0

Filmset by Pioneer, Perthshire
Printed in Great Britain by
St. Edmundsbury Press, Bury St. Edmunds, Suffolk

*To Christine for putting my
flannels and socks in the
washing machine with her red blouse.*

Contents

Acknowledgements

My thanks to Guildford Borough Records Office for letting me have a copy of the Court Book entry of 17 January 1598; Hugh Barty-King for the extract from *Quilt Winders and Pod Shavers;* Collins for the extract from Sir Arthur Bryant's *The Age of Elegance;* Sarah Potter for allowing me to use her quote on women and cricket; Frank Keating for a few lines from his writing on P. G. H. Fender and Bob Willis; John Woodcock for a paragraph on intimidating bowling; Jock Livingston for his story about a curious umpiring decision; Keith Miller for the umpire stories from *Cricket Crossfire;* Granada Publishing for the extracts from Hugh de Selincourt's *The Game of The Season;* Faber & Faber for the lines from Siegfried Sassoon's *Memoirs of a Fox-Hunting Man;* George Sassoon for the verse of Siegfried Sassoon's 'Dreamers'; Mary Evans for the Spofforth illustration; the BBC Hulton Picture Library for the picture of 'Ranji'; and particularly to Ossie, that is, H. A. Osborne Esq., the Sussex County Cricket Club's Honorary Librarian for help and his seemingly endless enthusiasm. Every effort has been made to make sure that everyone who should be acknowledged, has been. For any omissions, my apologies and a promise that the matter will be put right in future editions.

Why Nurdle?

Anyone who has seen a good village cricketer nurdle one round to leg and all along the ground knows that special feeling. It is contentment. It is a sight best seen through half-closed eyes, from the comfort of a deckchair. It brings not a roar from some mounded stand, but merely a murmur of knowing approval from benches and rugs. It is a moment when eyes, hands, feet, balance and timing come together, not in some mighty loft over the ropes for six, nor in a musketeer's delicate late cut for four. It is the one shot that, for a moment, was as good as any played by the greatest in the greatest game of them all.

One afternoon, on the bank of a fast river, the gillie referred not to the salmon, but to The Fish. So it is with cricket; it is not simply a game. Cricket is The Game.

I got my first bat, and a hero, almost forty years ago. The year was 1947. The hero, who I had not even seen, was Compton. For him 1947 was a wonderful season. He scored eighteen centuries and I was going to be D. C. S. Compton. In Dorman's, the village shop, I saw the bat. A real three-springer, it was a white smooth blade just waiting to hit eighteen hundreds, with a red-rubber covered handle and a small piece of postcard upon which was written 'Bat 11/-'. Eleven shillings! I was six and not even at Christmas had I ever seen eleven shillings. All I had in my money box was three shillings and eleven pence. Everyday I went into Dorman's and asked Mr Dorman if the bat was for sale and how much was it. Everyday, and very solemnly, he told me that it was and that it was eleven shillings exactly. It was that year that I learned to pray. For my family it was a trying time. We usually met at supper and every day without fail I would ask, as if for the first time, did they know that Mr Dorman had a bat for sale? The

Driver, it was called. How long would it take to save to eleven shillings? And, were there any jobs to be done, for tuppence? And then one morning, on the way to school, I saw the empty window. The Bat had gone. 'Sold,' said Mr Dorman. The misery continued right to Christmas morning. The Driver, the three-springer, with its red handle, appeared at the foot of my bed. A *real* three-springer and the most snow-bound winter of all to get through! The long passage from front door to kitchen became Lord's, the Oval and Canterbury. I was always Compton, although the confines of the narrow hallway never allowed a sweep on one knee. It did, however, mean that I was the only boy in the class who could play a perfectly straight bat; fact was, the winter restrictions of that hallway meant that the straight bat was about the only stroke I had!

And so my love of cricket was born. Like thousands of other youngsters, I never became D. C. S. Compton (despite buying Brylcreem for a while), but as a young man I started to travel the

PLAYER'S CIGARETTES

D. C. S. COMPTON

world and played cricket in Australia, New Zealand, America, China and even the Soviet Union, with a group known as the Moscow Cricket Club. I discovered that The Game was a bond. I found more than just companionship; there was a common cynicism towards the antics and sometimes the motives of the professional game. Many cricket followers are reactionaries, which is no bad thing, except that modern players are not reactionaries. I discovered also that lovers of The Game are often far more interested in records and statistics than other sports fans. This enthusiasm for the fastest fifties, the most wickets, the highest scores etc, would appear to reject the notion fostered by many close to the workings and commercialism of cricket, that the history of The Game is of little interest.

The introduction of a seemingly never ending diet of one day internationals and eliminating bouts, has encouraged the view that the modern approach is that which interests most people. To my (reactionary?) mind, however, the heart of The Game is to be found in non-league village cricket. Village cricket lives still, in spite of what has been claimed by many knowledgable writers and experts, and there exists alongside it, an enormous amount of good, clever and often amusing writing which echoes the heartbeat of The Game.

This writing is largely fact. The cricket novel is rare. The Game has inspired interludes in fiction, but few writers have cared to base a book on the flannelled sport. My shelves have supported some of the most magical characters, the most dramatic passages and the sweetest narratives — all of which has been non-fiction. The Game has provided the widest selection of people, settings and synopses without the writer having to resort to fantasy.

Some of the drama, intrigue, fun and excitement might be modern, but looking through the shelves I feel there is a tendency to neglect the older writings. There is often an impression given by those close to The Game and its literature that everybody in the world knows about Beldham and Lambert, the origin of Lord's, Reynell Cotton, Lang, Our Village, Hugh de Selincourt, Ponsonby-Fane and how Hendren came across a fellow with his throat cut in an Australian train. The truth is that most do not. Preparing and selecting the following passages from my shelves I spent much time reading them aloud to friends who are also

3

cricketers or fellow enthusiasts. I was pleasantly surprised by the number for whom a lot of the selections were quite new. Although they had heard about the passage from *England, Their England,* they had never actually read it. Others were meeting for the first time the story of Willes and the start of over-arm bowling.

The stories that interested people most were those about the origins of cricket and the tales from the nineteenth and early twentieth centuries. During the past twenty years an enormous quantity of modern cricketing biographies and Test Match specials have tumbled forth to the bookshops, which although they are wonderful have neglected the history of The Game. So, there is not much to be found in the following pages about modern cricket (yet I have included a splendid one-liner by E. W. Swanton on my hero, Compton).

The reader may find the selection whimsical. If it is, it is because for me The Game is whimsical. The origins, the characters, the often unbending leadership, its anachronisms and above all the sense of contentment that in the long run overcomes the frustrations. It is this contentment that is largely responsible for the title. I was at the Oval at the end of last season watching Sussex quietly thrash Surrey. Sitting alongside me was a silver-haired old gentleman whose playing days were clearly over but who had, apparently, been something of a wicket keeper and, of all things, a trombonist. Every so often he would nod off, clearly having had a good lunch. Sussex were batting, and I think it was Greig who picked a ball off his pads and gently turned it down to the fine leg boundary. The old fellow next to me, stirred gently and muttered, 'Nicely nurdled, Sir! Nicely nurdled.'

And with a contented smile he nodded off once more, safe in the knowledge that his team were on their way to victory.

I think for him, and to all those with such an uncomplicated love of The Game, these passages should be dedicated.

CHAPTER ONE

Creckett and other Plaies

The earliest sure record of cricket is said to be contained in the Guildford Borough Records. In the Court Book covering the years 1586 to 1675 is the claim that cricket was played at the Royal Grammar School in about 1550. Here is the relevant section for 17 January 1598:

> Court Leet held there Monday next after the Feast of St Hilary the fortieth year of the reign of our Lady Elizabeth, Queen of England, France and Ireland, Defender of the Faith etc.
>
> Memo. that att this day came John Derrick of Guldeford aforesaid gent one of the Queenes Majestes Coroners of the County of Surrey beinge of the age of fyfty and nyne yeeres or thereabouts and voluntarily sworne and examined saith upon his oath that he hath known the parcell of land lately used for a garden and sometimes in the occupacon of John Pavishe late of Guldeford aforesaid Inhoulder deceased lyinge in the parishe of the Holy Trinity in Guldeford aforesaid beteene the garden somtymes Thomas Northall on the north parte and the high way leadinge through the North Towne ditch of the said Towne of Guldeford on the south parte for the space of fyfty yeeres and more. And did knowe that the same lay waste and was used and occupied by the Inhabitantes of Guldeford aforesaid to lay Timber in and for sawpittes and for makinge of frames of Timber for the said Inhabitantes And that ould Butler a carpenter deceased dwellinge in the Towne aforesaid did commonly use to make frames of Timber there. And also this deponent saith that hee being a scholler in the free Schoole of Guldeford hee and divers of his fellowes did runne and play

5

there at Creckett and other Plaies And also that the same was used for the Baytinge of Beares in the said Towne untill the said John Parvishe did inclose the said parcell of land

And here is one George Swinnocke writing in 1672:

Maidstone was formerly a very prophane town, insomuch that (before 1640) I have seen morris-dancing cudgel-playing, stool-ball, crickets, and many other sports openly and publikly on the Lord's Day.

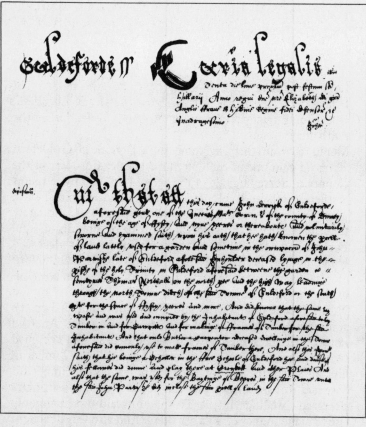

A page from the Guildford Borough Records showing cricket to have been played in the 1550s

Some have tried to show a connection with stool-ball mentioned by Swinnocke and cricket. Stool-ball is played today, especially in the south of England and has very similar Laws although it is played with a paddle bat. The 'stumps' consist of a square board on a pole at about head height. However, unless Swinnocke was referring here to cricket-fighting (ie 'ferocious' insects in a cage as recorded in parts of Asia), then the two sports were quite distinct in the second half of the seventeenth century.

There followed a series of sightings of The Game, including this note kept by the Chaplain of a group of warships:

> On May 6, 1976, this morning early, at least forty of the English, with his worship the Consull, rod out of the cytty about four miles to the Greene Platt, a fine vally by the river syde, to recreate themselves, where a princely tent was pitched: and we had severall pastimes and sports, as duck-hunting, fishing, shooting, hand-ball, krickett, scrofilo; and then a noble dinner brought thither with greate plenty of all sorts of wines, punch, and lemonade and at six wee returne all home in good order, but soundly tyred and weary.

Sounds like any other village game.

By 1705 there was no doubting that cricket was a very recognisable sport by today's standards:

> This is to give notice that a match of cricket is to be plaid between 11 gentlemen of the west part of the County of Kent, against as many of Chatham for 11 guineas a man at Maulden in Kent, on August 7th next.
>
> *The Postman*, Kent, 1705

As I have said, the early reports suggest that cricket was established in the south of England, in Guildford, or Guldeford as it was, spreading to Kent, Sussex and Hampshire. The most famous surviving name of those early days was Hambledon. One Richard Hayes records in June 1776:

> I set off about seven in the morning to Sevenoaks Vine to see Hambledon play with All England at cricket. The Duke of Dorset bowled the first four balls. . . . The Duke was

7

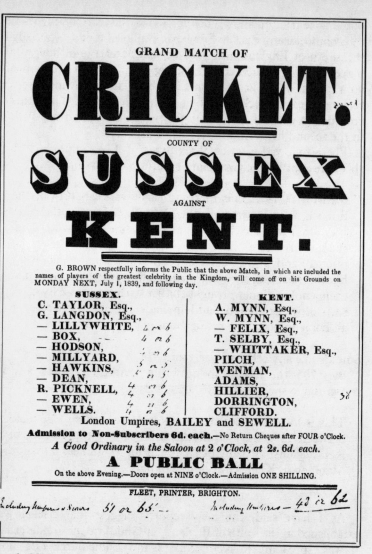

GRAND MATCH OF

CRICKET.

COUNTY OF

SUSSEX

AGAINST

KENT.

G. BROWN respectfully informs the Public that the above Match, in which are included the names of players of the greatest celebrity in the Kingdom, will come off on his Grounds on MONDAY NEXT, July 1, 1839, and following day.

SUSSEX.

C. TAYLOR, Esq.,
G. LANGDON, Esq.,
— LILLYWHITE, *4 or 6*
— BOX, *4 or 6*
— HODSON, *4 or 6*
— MILLYARD, *5 or 6*
— HAWKINS, *5 or 5*
— DEAN, *5 or 5*
R. PICKNELL, *4 or 6*
— EWEN, *4 or 6*
— WELLS. *4 or 6*

KENT.

A. MYNN, Esq.,
W. MYNN, Esq.,
— FELIX, Esq.,
T. SELBY, Esq.,
— WHITTAKER, Esq.,
PILCH,
WENMAN,
ADAMS,
HILLIER, *38*
DORRINGTON,
CLIFFORD.

London Umpires, **BAILEY** and **SEWELL.**

Admission to Non-Subscribers 6d. each.—No Return Cheques after FOUR o'Clock.

A Good Ordinary in the Saloon at 2 o'Clock, at 2s. 6d. each.

A PUBLIC BALL

On the above Evening.—Doors open at NINE o'Clock.—Admission ONE SHILLING.

FLEET, PRINTER, BRIGHTON.

Including Umpires & Scorers 51 or 65... Including Umpires — 43 or 62

A. Mynn, seen here in the Kent team, had been condemned to having his leg amputated just a few years earlier (see. p. 18)

bowled out after getting about six runs. I heard him say if he missed a ball he was sure to be out. The Hambledon men were in between five and six hours. They beat us in guarding

8

their wickets and in standing out too. *N.B.* They talk of having three stumps. By their playing with very broad bats and playing all the blocking short play, so that it is a very hard matter to hit a wicket.

Three stumps instead of two! Some thought it unfair. This report from the *Kentish Gazette* suggests that two stumps had indeed been hard to hit:

On Sevenoaks Vine on Wednesday 18th June instant will be played the first match for a thousand guineas. Hampshire against All England. The wickets to be pitched at ten o'clock and to be played with three stumps to shorten the game.

Kentish Gazette, 4 June 1777

The idea of using three stumps certainly appeared two years before the Sevenoaks game. John Nyren the cricket chronicler of the famous Hambledon team, recorded an occasion when it was decided that hitting two stumps (or one of them) was too difficult.

Surrey cricket ground in 1848. The only recognizable thing today is the church.

On the 22nd of May 1775, a match was played in the Artillery Ground, between five of the Hambledon Club and five of All England; when Small went in the last man for fourteen runs, and fetched them. Lumpy was bowler upon the occasion; and it having been remarked that his balls had three several times passed between Small's stumps, it was considered to be a hard thing upon the bowler that his straightest balls should be thus sacrificed; the number of the stumps was in consequence increased from two to three.

Nearly a hundred years later the bowlers were still complaining. And so in 1872 in Lancashire, during a two-day match between Manchester and Birkenhead Park, four stumps were placed at either end . . . they still couldn't hit them! Perhaps, more accurately, it was recognised that adding an extra stump would make little or no difference to first-class players. Whatever the reason, the experiment succeeded in convincing the powers-that-were that three sticks were better than four. (Interesting to note that the powers at the time all fancied themselves as batsmen.)

G. T. Knight, a nineteenth-century All-England player, was also a writer on bowling styles. He had plenty to say about the size of the wicket. Here he is writing in about 1828:

The object is not to bring the batting down to the bowling in order to equalize them, but to exalt the latter to the level of the former; not to diminish the means of defence, but to add to the powers of the attack. A wicket may be extended to the size of a gate, or a bat diminished to that of a walking-stick; and at some intermediate point, there is no doubt but that men may be got out with tolerable certainty, just as a log of sufficient weight will reduce the speed of a racehorse to that of a pig.

A year earlier, Knight had played in an important trial of styles. There had been considerable anger at the idea that bowlers might move from underarm to roundarm. A three-match trial between Sussex and All-England was fixed to test the caddish roundarm bowling. The old style of underarm had been conquered by the batsmen and many of them viewed the modern method, which they regarded as throwing, with considerable

10

alarm. In fact, in 1827, a group of the All-England players threatened to pull out of the game with Sussex because the southern side bowled the new and 'unfair' way. Here is their ultimatum:

> We the undersigned do agree, that we will not play the third match between All-England and Sussex, which is intended to be at Brighton, in July or August, unless the Sussex players bowl fair; that is, abstain from THROWING. T. Marsden, W. Ashby, W. Matthews, W. Searle, J. Saunders, T. C. Howard, W. Caldecourt, F. Pilch, T. Beagley.

But they did play.

A young man called John Willes is said to be the one responsible for starting bowlers on the way to roundarm and eventually overarm bowling. Undoubtedly others had tried to vary their bowling, including Tom Walker of Hambledon and the eminent Nottingham bowler, William Clarke. Years before Willes, Walker had been banned for 'throwing'. Willes however kept at it and, according to cricket legend, was supported by his sister. His sister? Try imagining a young lady in early voluminous eighteenth-century frocks attempting to bowl straightforward underarm and you'll soon see that the young lady's hand would have had to have come up to avoid her enormous skirts. A. G. Steel, the Lancashire player and, later, President of the M.C.C., wrote this comment on John Willes in the Badminton Library Edition of *Cricket,* published in the late 1880s:

> Mr. Willes, being a most enthusiastic cricketer, and not content with the summer months for his favourite sport, used in the winter daily to repair to his barn, and there measure out the proper distance, pitch the stumps, and, with his sister (also an enthusiast) as bowler, enjoy a good practice. Now every one who has seen ladies attempting to throw a stone or cricket ball will remember that they invariably have a half-round, half-under sort of delivery, and this Miss Willes, in common with the majority of ladies, seems to have possessed. Her brother, acustomed to play against what in those days was the only known style of bowling, viz., under-arm, was somewhat perplexed and

11

worried with this unknown feminine species of ball, which doubtless he found difficult to tackle. We are not told whether his feelings of shame at being thus defeated, or of delight at discovering this new style of bowling, predominated, but we ARE told that shortly afterwards he made his DEBUT as a round-arm bowler, and met with (until he was stopped by the conservatism of the crowd) the greatest success.

By 1864, the bowling mafia had overcome the objections. The debate had been quite traumatic; from underarm, to roundarm, to overarm, had been a revolution indeed according to The Hon. R. H. Lyttleton writing a review of major changes in the game, in the nineteenth century:

Since 1827 the only noteworthy revolution which has taken place was in 1864, when the bowler was allowed to deliver the ball with his arm above the shoulder, a most important concession, only granted at the time after fierce opposition. The bowling of Spofforth at his fastest, Ulyett, Mr. Rotherham and others on the old-fashioned wickets, before the introduction of the mowing-machine and a heavy roller, would have prevented heavy run-getting by the simple expedient of severely injuring the batsman — not a desirable method by any means. But the new rule for a time somewhat diminished scores, and only ceased to be more efficacious as the grounds improved. As far as bowling is concerned things have not altered since, and it is impossible that any further change can take place, as public opinion has spoken out strongly in regard to throwing, which owing to the weakness of umpires and the great laxity of cricket committees crept into vogue a few years ago.

*

But cricket like any other surviving fancy is about people, not laws. The early cricketers appear to have been men of great character, even if individuals sometimes displayed dubious sides to their nature. The gentry and their followers amused themselves

12

with cricket; it was a sport for prestige and, very often, large wagers. Eric Parker, in his *History of Cricket*, makes the point that the Oaks, the Derby and the M.C.C. were established in the same decade of each other (between 1780 and 1787). The suggestion is that cricket was very much part of the gambling scene and, indeed, thousands of pounds were put on matches. (More of which later.)

The famous names of the time included a fair sprinkling of the aristocracy and their gamekeepers. Some of the latter were poached in order that the duke or the baronet might improve his cricketing reputation. One character, straight from an early chocolate box cover of clay pipes and hunting pink was Squire Osbaldeston. He was a hearty huntsman and an enthusiastic cricketer. He recorded in his memoirs some wonderful portraits of the tough southern cricketers of the late eighteenth and early nineteenth centuries. Here he is writing about Lambert and Budd. Lambert was a Surrey man, born in 1779 and said to have been one of the finest batsmen, bowlers and fielders of his time. He partnered Squire Osbaldeston in many a hitting and bowling contest. E. H. Budd was thought to be the strongest bowler of his day . . .

As wicket-keeper, fieldsman, bowler and batter, no man ever equalled Lambert. Apropos bat, batting and catching, Mr. Budd was the hardest hitter I ever saw; several times he hit the ball over the palings without touching them. In one match Lambert was bowling and Mr. Budd caught the ball a half-volley, hitting it as hard as he did when he sent it over the palings, and Lambert caught it with one hand, throwing it up as if he had taken it out of his pocket. The eye could only follow the ball for half a second and then it was out of sight.

. . . Lambert was the first to discover I was so fast a bowler. Lord Frederick Beauclerc, a first-rate player, very long-headed and a great judge of the game, was not then aware that I could bowl so great a pace, and by the advice of Lambert I made a match to play against Lord Frederick and Howard; the latter not so fast a bowler as I was, but steadier. Some time before the match came off I was taken very ill and was confined to my room. I wrote to Lord Frederick, informing him of my situation and saying how obliged I should be to him if he would consent to postpone the match. He wrote a very laconic answer back, declining my request, and I thought nothing then remained to be settled but a forfeit. I named this to Lambert, who came to see me. He said, 'I think if I could be allowed a fieldsman I could beat them both.' I told him I thought such an issue never could occur, but if he liked to try the experiment he should have the stakes if he won.

I applied for a fieldsman, but with the same result as attended my suggestion of postponement. Lambert then said that if I could only hit a ball and get a run he could claim a fieldsman. I told him I was so weak and reduced I could never accomplish it; but at his earnest desire I consented and went to Lord's in my carriage. Fully half the match was over and Lambert being just then out, I went in; but from the quantity of medicine I had taken, and being shockingly weak from long confinement to my room, I felt quite dizzy and faint. Lord Frederick bowled to me; luckily he was a slow bowler, and I could manage to get out of harm's way if necessary, but it did not so happen. I hit one of his balls so hard I had time to walk a run. He then became vexed and desired Howard [Lord Frederick's partner] to bowl; but I gave up my bat and claimed a fieldsman. This claim was not admitted. When I walked the run many of the spectators cheered, all the cricketers knowing the circumstances. The match was not over that day as Lord Frederick had to go in against Lambert's score. I attended and saw the issue, and was never more gratified in my life than I was when Lambert bowled his Lordship out and won the match.

Lambert was a bold, forward player according to the Rev. James Pycroft. He wrote as much in his book, *The Cricket Field*, which appeared in 1851 (coincidentally, the year of Lambert's death). The great single wicket contest between Osbaldeston and Lambert and Beauclerc and Howard was but one example of the enormous interest and equally large bets in and on the game. Pycroft recorded the views of E. H. Budd of another game in which there was said to have been some cheating so big were the financial stakes:

In 1817, we went, said Mr. Budd, with Osbaldston to play twenty-two of Nottingham. In that match Clarke played. In common with others, I lost my money, and was greatly disappointed at the termination. One paid player was accused of selling, and never employed after. The concourse of people was very great: these were the days of the Luddites (rioters), and the magistrates warned us, that unless we would stop our game at seven o'clock, they could not answer for keeping the peace. At seven o'clock we stopped; and, simultaneously, the thousands who lined the ground began to close in upon us. Lord Frederick lost nerve and was very much alarmed; but I said they didn't want to hurt us. No; they simply came to have a look at the eleven men who ventured to play two for one.

Both Lambert and Budd had adopted the roundarm technique of bowling. According to Pycroft, the style they followed belonged to the Nottingham slow bowler William Clarke. Here is Pycroft again, writing in the 1850s:

Lambert's bowling was like Mr. Budd's, against which I have often played: a high, underhand delivery, slow, but rising very high, very accurately pitched, and turning in from leg stump. 'About the year 1818, Lambert and I,' said Mr. Budd, 'attained to a kind of round-arm delivery (described as Clarke's), by which we rose decidedly superior to all the batsmen of the day. Mr. Ward could not play it, but he headed a party against us, and our new bowling was ignored.'

Another parson writer of things cricket, was the Rev. John Mitford. It is difficult to pick out only a single piece of Mitford, for the remainder should be read also, but I have a fondness for his description of William Beldham who was born in 1766 and died in 1862. There are those who say that if comparisons could be made, then Beldham would be judged the greatest cricketer of all.

But before Mitford's note on him, here is John Nyren's impression:

We used to call him 'Silver Billy'. No one within my recollection could stop a ball better, or make more brilliant hits all over the ground. Wherever the ball was bowled, there she was hit away, and in the most severe, venomous style. . . . One of the most beautiful sights that can be imagined, and which would have delighted an artist, was to see him make himself up to hit a ball. It was the beau ideal of grace, animation, and concentrated energy . . .

And now to Mitford: he said of Beldham, 'Michael Angelo should have painted him . . . he took the ball, as Burke did the House of Commons, between wind and water; not a moment too soon or late . . .'

But it is Mitford's portrait of Beldham in old age which is for me very special:

Beldham still survives. He lives near Farnham; and in his kitchen, black with age, but like himself, still untouched with worms, hangs the trophy of his victories; the delight of his youth, the exercise of his manhood, and the glory of his age — his BAT. Reader, believe me when I tell you I trembled when I touched it; it seemed an act of profaneness, of violation. I pressed it to my lips, and returned it to its sanctuary.

That moment captured by Mitford, suggests the very contentment prized and understood by followers of The Game. Beldham played at Hambledon, supposedly the cradle of cricket. Another splendid Hambledon man was David Harris, described by Andrew Lang (of whom, more later) as a 'Christian and cricketer'. John Nyren's description of Harris conjures a curious image for a man so fêted as a successful bowler:

His attitude when preparing for his run previously to delivering the ball would have made a beautiful study for the sculptor. First of all, he stood erect like a soldier at drill; then, with a graceful curve of the arm, he raised the ball to his forehead, and drawing back his right foot, started off with his left. His mode of delivering the ball was very singular. He would bring it from under the arm with a twist

16

and nearly as high as his arm-pit, and with this action PUSH it, as it were, from him. How it was that the balls acquired the velocity they did by this mode of delivery I never could comprehend.

In bowling, he never stooped in the least in his delivery, but kept himself upright all the time. His balls were very little beholden to the ground when pitched; it was but a touch, and up again; and woe to the man who did not get into block them, for they had such a peculiar curl, that they would grind his fingers against the bat: many a time have I seen blood drawn in this way from a batter who was not up to the trick; old Tom Walker was the only exception — I have before classed him among the bloodless animals.

Hambledon's men were famous for their stern cricket — although few were 'bloodless animals'. Many fancied themselves as singers and one particularly famous player was a violinist. His name was Small. John Nyren's description of the Artillery Ground match between five of the Hambledon Club and five of All-England, had Small as the last man in getting the fourteen needed runs. John Small was born in 1737. As with many of his kind, Small was something of a musician and an occasional poet. As a cricketer he was known throughout the land; certainly Small was regarded with some esteem as a player (with bat and fiddle) by one of the patrons of the game, the Duke of Dorset. The Duke sent Small a violin as a present and, it is recorded, 'paid the carriage'. It is appropriate that one of the best tributes to Small came in the form of a verse by Pierce Egan:

John Small (1737 – 1826)

Here lies, bowled out by Death's unerring ball,
A Cricketer renowned, by name John Small,
But though his name was Small, yet great his fame,
For nobly did he play the noble game;
His life was like his innings, long and good,
Full ninety summers he had death withstood.
At length the ninetieth winter came, when (fate
Not leaving him one solitary mate)
This last of Hambledonians, Old John Small,
Gave up his bat and ball, his leather, wax and all.

17

CHAPTER TWO

A Sovran Sport

Beldham, Small, Budd, Harris *et al.* were not only fine cricketers, they were tough men. In their day, protection for the batsman was minimal. Lord Frederick Beauclerc is said to have taken one look at the first pads, or leggings as they were called, and declared that they would never be used because they would be unfair. Sir Spencer Ponsonby-Fane, in a preface to *Lord's and the M.C.C.* in 1914, wrote:

> When leg-pads were first introduced they were worn *under* the trousers, as though the hardy cricketer was ashamed of his cowardice in wearing them . . .

In the early writings, there is much reference to the game being 'manly'. Certainly there were serious accidents, and not always to the players. Hugh Barty-King records in his *Quilt Winders and Pod Shavers*, two incidents: one to a bystander, the other to that enormous Kent player, Alfred Mynn. The first occurred during a match played at Ticehurst in Sussex in August 1825. A ball from the bat of Thomas Cooper was caught on the point of a knife which a woman named Stapley, who was running a ginger beer stall on the ground, happened to be holding in her hand at the time. 'Her hand was much cut by the involuntary feat,' reported *Bell's Life*, 'and the ball was so deeply perforated that some little force was found necessary to draw the knife from it . . .'

Alfred Mynn, protagonist of fast roundarm bowling, was himself an early victim of it at the wicket. At a game at Leicester in 1836 between North and South, Mynn was knocked down and severely injured by a ball from Samuel Redgate which hit his unpadded leg. He could not rise from the pitch. He was carefully lifted on to a stretcher packed round with splints, and placed on the roof of the stagecoach. On reaching London he felt unable to continue the journey to his home in Kent, and was taken to Bart's Hospital where he was examined by surgeons who told him they would have to amputate his thigh at the hip. Luckily they had second thoughts, and after an absence of two years Mynn returned to the cricket field and played as well as ever.

Frederick Prince of Wales was not so fortunate. A keen follower of cricket, his appearances as a player were often noted in the press:

> The great cricket match between H.R.H. the Prince of Wales for Surrey and London and Lord John Sackville, son of his Grace, the Duke of Dorset for Kent, was played on Kennington Common . . . the press was so great on the occasion that a poor woman, by the crowd bearing upon her, unfortunately had her leg broke, which being related to His Royal Highness, he was pleased to order her ten guineas.
>
> *London Evening Post*, 1737

An account of the cause of his death appears in *Wraxall's Memoirs*:

> Frederick, Prince of Wales, son of George II, expired suddenly in 1751, at Leicester House, in the arms of Desnoyers, the celebrated dancing master. His end was caused by an internal abscess that had long been forming in consequence of a blow which he received in the side from a cricket ball while he was engaged in playing at the game on the lawn at Cliefden House in Buckinghamshire, where he then principally resided. Death did not take place, however, till several months after the accident, when a collection of matter burst and instantly suffocated him.

Cricket has often been described as a dangerous game although until recent years nobody felt the need for the assorted pieces of high tensile armoury adopted by modern professional cricketers. That able chronicler, the Rev. James Pycroft writing in 1851 remembers:

> At Oxford I once could see, any day in summer, on Cowley Marsh, two rows of six wickets each facing some other, with

a space of about sixty yards between each row, and ten yards between each wicket. Then, you have twelve bowlers, aos à dos, and as many hitters — making twelve balls and twenty-four men, all in danger's way at once, besides by-standers. The most any one of these bowlers can do is to look out for the ball of his own set; whether hit or not by a ball from behind, is very much a matter of chance. A ball from the opposite row once touched my hair! The wonder is, that twelve balls should be flying in a small space nearly every day, yet no man hit in the face.

*

So what attracts people to the game? Leaving aside its dangerous aspects, it must also be one of the most inconvenient of sports. Even the casual knockabout needs plenty of fielders with enthusiasm enough to chase the ball without ever having the chance of a 'shot at goal'. And, as has often been noted, it is an unforgiving sport, especially for the batsman. The opening bat, with his guards and padding to protect him and his average and reputation at stake, can too easily be out first ball. The soccer forward will quickly get another chance to score, the tennis star to correct his service and even the tumbling jockey may get to ride a winner in the next race. For the batsman, however, out is out. Yet the same batsman on form might condemn the bowler to a day, perhaps three days, of utter misery. As for the fielder and his dropped catch . . . ! But cricket is about optimism. Optimism which comes from the supporters as well as the players and which is, perhaps, a peculiar trait of the English. Charles Box, commenting in 1877 on *The English Game of Cricket* wrote:

In no other country but England would the attack and defence of three stumps be witnessed by enormous crowds of fashionable people with unflagging zest, and there are not many foreigners as yet who would care to face a swift bowler with no other protection than a bat.

Andrew Lang has a simple assessment of the game:

20

Cricket is simply the most catholic and diffused, the most innocent, kindly and manly of popular pleasures, while it has been the delight of statesmen and the relaxation of learning.

I think I would have liked to have been Andrew Lang. He was born in 1844, just five years after the formation of the finest of all county cricket clubs, Sussex. He was a wonderful illustration of the all round man — often the mark of a good cricketer. An historian, a classicist and a poet. His writing is a reminder that Scottish cricket has its own history. A few years before his death in 1912, Lang recalled the first time he had seen The Game: it was in the Borders — a long way indeed from the established south coast wickets.

The first time I ever saw bat and ball must have been about 1850. The gardener's boy and his friends were playing with home-made bats, made out of firwood with the bark on, and with a gutta-percha ball. The game instantly fascinated me, and when I once understood why the players ran after

making a hit, the essential difficulties of comprehension were overcome. Already the border towns, Hawick, Kelso, Selkirk, Galashiels, had their elevens. To a small boy the spectacle of the various red and blue caps and shirts was very delightful. The grounds were, as a rule very rough and bad. Generally the play was on haughs, level pieces of town-land beside the rivers. Then the manufacturers would encroach on the cricket-field, and build a mill on it, and cricket would have to seek new settlements.

In these early days, when one was only a small spectator, say, and in later days too, the great difficulty of cricket was that excellent thing in itself, too much patriotism. Almost the whole population of a town would come to the ground and take such a keen interest in the fortunes of their side, that the other side, if it won, was in some danger of rough handling. Probably no one was ever much hurt; indeed, the squabbles were rather a sham fight than otherwise; but still, bad feeling was caused by umpires' decisions. Then relations would be broken off between the clubs of different towns, and sometimes this tedious hostility endured for years . . .

Badminton Library of Sports and Pastimes

Later, in the same article, Lang wrote:

Our wickets keep falling in this life. One after the other goes down. They are becoming few who joined in those Border matches where there was but one lazy spectator, when we made such infrequent runs, and often dropped a catch, but never lost heart, never lost pleasure in the game. Some of them may read this, and remember old friends gone, old games played, old pewters drained, old pipes smoked, old stories told, remember the leg-hitting of Jack Grey, the bowling of Bill Dryden and of Clement Glassford, the sturdy defence of William Forman. And he who writes, recalling that simple delight and good fellowship, recalling those kind faces and merry days in the land of Walter Scott, may make his confession, and may say that such years were worth living for, and that neither study, nor praise, nor any other pleasure has equalled, or can equal, the joy of having been young and a cricketer . . .

22

And so to Lang the poet and his Ballade of Cricket:

Ballade of Cricket
by
Andrew Lang

The burden of hard hitting; slog away!
Here shall thou make a 'five' and there a 'four',
And then upon thy bat shall lean, and say,
That thou art in for an uncommon score.
Yea, the loud ring applauding thee shall roar,
And thou to rival Thornton shalt aspire;
When lo, the Umpire gives thee 'leg before' —
'This is the end of every man's desire.'
The burden of much bowling, when the stay
Of all thy team is 'collared', swift and slower,
When 'bailers' break not in their wonted way,
And 'yorkers' come not off as here-to-fore;
When length balls shoot no more — ah never more!
When all deliveries lose their former fire,
When bats seem broader than the broad barn-door —
'This is the end of every man's desire.'
The burden of long fielding, when the clay
Clings to thy shoon in sudden shower's downpour,
And running still thou stumblest; or the ray
Of blazing suns doth bite and burn thee sore,
And blind thee till, forgetful of thy lore,
Thou dost most mournfully misjudge a 'skyer',
And lose a match the Fates cannot restore —
'This is the end of every man's desire.'
Envoy
Alas, yet liefer on Youth's hither shore
Would I be some poor Player on scant hire,
Than king among the old who play no more, —
'THIS is the end of every man's desire.'

As Lang says, it is better to be the poorest player than not to play
at all. As many a frustrated village skipper will know, the poorest
player is often the most resilient, the most thick-skinned to jibes

and looks that suggest that when it comes to skill, something may be lacking. Perhaps it is to do with having nothing to lose.

E. V. Lucas knew all about the place of the cricketing hopeless — and hopeful — and Hazlitt knew the spell of cricket over Englishmen:

> There is no other game at which the confirmed duffer is so persistent and so undepressed. It is for the experts, victims of misfortune, that depression awaits; it is they who chew the cud of bitterness.
>
> E. V. Lucas

> The very names of cricket bat and ball make English fingures tingle.
>
> William Hazlitt

Now why should fingers tingle? Long summer afternoons? Lazy days? Home county sandwiches on soft rugs at Third Man? Worcester's tall spire? Here is good caution from J. B. Priestley reminding us that although cricket may have been nursed in the south, some of its most able players and knowing spectators are northeners — yet Englishmen of course:

> In spite of recent jazzed-up matches, cricket to be fully appreciated demands leisure, some sunny warm days, and an understanding of its finer points — and it depends more than any other ball game on varying conditions, on the state of the pitch, on weather and wind and light, it multiplies its fine points. Though it is often considered a 'gentlemanly game', an idea supported by its leisurely progress and breaks for lunch, tea, cool drinks on the field, we must remember that many of its greatest performers came from the Industrial North, which also supplied, until our own time, large numbers of its most knowledgeable and keenest spectators.
>
> J. B. Priestley, *The English*, 1973

North or south, it mattered not to the historian Sir Arthur Bryant. In his *The Age of Elegance*, Sir Arthur had a simple explanation of the connection between cricket and the English character, particularly The Game's ability to cross social lines:

'Nothing,' the Duke of Wellington declared, 'the people of this country like so much as to see their great men take part in their amusements; the aristocracy will commit a great error if ever they fail to mix freely with their neighbours ...'

On the cricket field too, the conventions of rank were forgotten; the best man was 'the hardest swipe, the most active field, the stoutest bowler.' 'Who that has been at Eton,' asked the author of the *English Spy*, 'has not repeatedly heard Jem Powell in terms of exultation cry, "Only see me liver this here ball, my young master"?' The game was played by the Prince Regent — before he let down his belly — on his ground at Brighton, by the aristocracy who liked to gamble over it, and by the young farmers and labourers of almost every south country village.

Mary Russell Mitford writing of eighteenth-century English village life and its cricketers, was quite certain that if nothing else, cricket and industry went together:

Note that your good cricketer is commonly the most industrious man in the parish; the habits that make him

such are precisely those which make a good workman —
steadiness, sobriety, and activity.

In more modern times, the recognition of cricket's place in the
way of British life was shown during the Second World War
when a series of essays was published by the British Council. As
the Earl of Derby wrote in the foreword to the collection:

No description of British life could fail to take account of
sport . . . Almost every other game of sport with which we
entertain ourselves belongs also today to many other
countries, but cricket, that defence of two citadels of three
stumps apiece against the missile of a ball, has never taken
root anywhere save in English-speaking countries, and so it
is our most typically national game . . .
   The stranger is apt to make his first acquaintance with
cricket at a big match, possibly at Lord's ground in London
. . . It is certain that he will hear with some amazement that
this match occupies three days. He will wonder how there
are so many people who can afford to be idle, and secondly
how they can be satisfied for long spells of time with so little
action.
   Surely he will think they must be held there by some
singular magic and he had best accept that view until he has
watched for some little while and come to feel the spell
himself . . . Fascinating it must be, for once the spectator
has settled down in the sunshine, he is most unwilling to go
away. He declares virtuously that he must go, that he will
stay only another five minutes, ten minutes, quarter of an
hour. The big clock ticks out those minutes relentlessly;
there is no pretence that he cannot see it, and still he
remains as the day wears on and the shadows of the players
grow longer. There is always some temptation to remain, to
see if a batsman reaches a particular score or, should he
depart, to see how his successor will fare. And cricket is
essentially a sunshine game. In its nature it cannot be played
in time of tempest. Like a sundial it only counts the sunny
hours and as soon as the raindrops fall the white figures
vanish . . .

The sunny hours are the best to remember and cricketers tend to have long, if convenient, memories. The Rev. Reynell Cotton in 1772 put his adoration of what even he called an old *English* sport into verse:

Cricket
by
Reynell Cotton

Assist, all ye Muses, and join to rehearse
An old English sport, never praised yet in verse:
'Tis Cricket I sing, of illustrious fame,
No nation e'er boasted so noble a game.
  Derry down, etc.
Great Pindar has bragg'd of his heroes of old —
Some were swift in the race, some in battles were bold:
The brows of the victor with olive were crown'd:
Hark! they shout, and Olympia returns the glad sound.
What boasting of Castor and Pollux his brother,
The one famed for riding, for boxing the other;
Compar'd with our heroes they'll not shine at all —
What were Castor and Pollux to Nyren and Small?
Here's guarding and catching, and throwing and tossing,
And bowling and striking and running and crossing;
Each mate must excel in some principal part —
The Pentathlum of Greece could not show so much art.
Ye bowlers, take heed, to my precepts attend;
On you the whole fate of the game must depend;
Spare your vigour at first, now exert all your strength.
But measure each step, and be sure pitch a length.
Ye fieldsmen, look sharp, lest your pains ye beguile;
Move close like an army, in rank and in file;
When the ball is return'd, back it sure, for I trow
Whole states have been ruin'd by one overthrow.
Ye strikers, observe when the foe shall draw nigh;
Mark the bowler, advancing with vigilant eye;
Your skill all depends upon distance and sight,
Stand firm to your scratch, let your bat be upright.
Buck, Curry and Hogsflesh, and Barbour and Brett,
Whose swiftness in bowling was ne'er equalled yet;

I had almost forgot, they deserve a large bumper,
Little George, the longstop, and Tom Sueter, the stumper.
Then why should we fear either Sackville or Mann,
Or repine at the loss both of Boynton and Lann?
With such troops as those we'll be lords of the game,
Spite of Minshull and Miller and Lumpy and Frame.
Then fill up your glass, he's the best that drinks most.
Here's the Hambledon Club! Who refuses the toast?
Let's join in the praise of the bat and the wicket,
And sing in full chorus the patrons of cricket.
And when the game's o'er, and our fate shall draw nigh
(For the heroes of cricket, like others, must die),
Our bats we'll resign, neither troubled nor vex'd,
And give up our wickets to those who come next.
    Derry down, etc.

Maybe some cricketers will give up their wickets to those who
come next, but many are often reluctant to give up anything —
even when they are given out by that most impartial of all
referees, the Umpire. For most cricketers there is always next
season, and whose heart could not open to the dreams of bat and
ball when Edmund Blunden writes as he does in part of his 'The
Season Opens':

And now where the confident cuckoo takes flight
Over buttercups kindled in millions last night,
A labourer leans on the stackyard's low wall
With the hens bothering round him, and dreams bat and
     ball;
Till the meadow is quick with the masters who were,
And he hears his own shouts when he first trotted there;
Long ago; all gone home now; but here they come all!
Surely these are the same, who now bring bat and ball?

More verse: H. S. Vere Hodge in 'Chant Royal of Cricket',
knew all about that hope that comes in May when a real young
man's fancy turns also to The Game. Naturally, the poet knew
also of the three-sweater start to practically every season, but let
us not spoil the image of the 'Sovran King of Sport':

Chant Royal
of Cricket
by
H. S. V. Hodge

When earth awakes as from some dreadful night
  And doffs her melancholy mourning state,
When May buds burst in blossom and requite
  Our weary eyes for Winter's tedious wait,
Then the pale bard takes down his dusty lyre
And strikes the thing with more than usual fire.
Myself, compacted of an earthier clay
I oil my bats and greasy homage pay
  To Cricket, who, with emblems of his court,
Stumps, pads, bails, gloves, begins his summer sway.
  Cricket in sooth is Sovran King of Sport.

As yet no shadows blur the magic light,
  The glamour that surrounds the opening date.
Illusions yet undashed my soul excite
  And of success in luring whispers prate.
I see myself in form: my thoughts aspire
To reach the giddy summit of desire.
Lovers and such may sing a roundelay,
Whate'er that be, to greet returning May;
  For me, not much — the season's all too short;
I hear the mower hum and scent the fray.
  Cricket in sooth is Sovran King of Sport.

A picture stands before my dazzled sight,
  Wherein the hero, ruthlessly elate,
Defies all bowlers' concentrated spire.
  That hero is myself, I need not state.
'Tis sweet to see their captain's growing ire
And his relief when I at last retire;
'Tis sweet to run pavilionwards and say,
'Yes, somehow I WAS seeing them today' —
  Thus Modesty demands that I retort
To murmured compliments upon my play.
  Cricket in sooth is Sovran King of Sport.

The truth's resemblance is, I own, but slight
    To these proud visions which my soul inflate.
This is the sort of thing: In abject fright
    I totter down the steps and through the gate;
Somehow I reach the pitch and bleat, 'Umpire,
Is that one leg?' What boots it to enquire?
The impatient bowler takes one grim survey,
Speeds to the crease and whirls — a lightning ray?
    No, a fast yorker. Bang! the stumps cavort.
Chastened, but not surprised, I go my way.
    Cricket in sooth is Sovran King of Sport.

Lord of the Game, for whom these lines I write,
    Fulfil my present hope, watch o'er my fate;
Defend me from the swerver's puzzling flight;
    Let me not be run out, at any rate.
As one who's been for years a constant trier,
Reward me with an average slightly higher;
Let it be double figures. This I pray,
Humblest of boons, before my hair grows grey
    And Time's flight bids me in the last resort
Try golf, or otherwise your cause betray.
    Cricket in sooth is Sovran King of Sport.

King, what though Age's summons I obey,
Resigned to dull rheumatics and decay,
    Still on one text my hearers I'll exhort,
As long as hearers within range will stay,
    'Cricket in sooth is Sovran King of Sport'.

*

There is something in the thought that cricket was invented to
infuriate foreigners. This was at one time considered a reasonable
idea when most Englishmen believed that all modern civilization
rested in these islands.

    George Macaulay Trevelyan once noted that disinterested
intellectual curiosity is the life blood of real civilization. On
reflection this is perhaps why cricket spectators are generally such
civilized folk. Civilized attitudes include the ability to sit alongside

one another through a three day county game and never be bored with the match nor with each others company. Trevelyan pitied the French nobility for not understanding this. He wrote:

> If the French noblesse had been capable of playing cricket with their peasants, their chateaux would never have been burnt.

Geoffrey Moorhouse writing in 1979 in *The Best Loved Game* has a similar dig at the French:

> I'm not at all surprised the French have never understood this game, whose players cannot be *serieux* when their honour is at stake.

But it is not only the French who have difficulties comprehending Le Game. Herbert Farjeon explained why Americans have as much trouble understanding cricket as the rest of the world has with American football:

> Americans don't appreciate cricket because they don't understand it.
> 'What in thunder is everybody laughing at?' the American cries.
> You tell him.
> The wicket keeper is running after the ball. The umpire is nearly killed. The batsman has bruised his toe. The spectators thought a run was going to be scored and it wasn't. The face of the American remains impassive. Even when you tell facts like these, he does not laugh.
> Well, well, he is young yet. It takes generations to see the joke of cricket.

Joke? It is not always clear, especially when The Game is taken so seriously. Sometimes the joke is told by cricket itself. It may, as the historian suggested, be a great leveller; cricket is a transparent cape under which no character is anonymous. Neville Cardus knew this when he followed the philosophy of 'what's bred in the bone will come out at cricket'. In this piece of what is my favourite Cardus, he writes of Tyldesley who played for

Lancashire in the 1920s and the Oxford and M.C.C. man, the Hon C. N. Bruce, later the third Lord Abedare:

A true batsman should in most of his strokes tell the truth about himself. An innings by Lord Aberdare comes straight out of Debrett's. And an innings by Richard Tyldesley comes straight out of Westhoughton. The accent in each case is true. If Tyldesley were to flash his left leg over to the off and drive a ball through the covers with Lord Aberdare's aristocratic pose it would be as false as if the man himself came to me and said; 'I beg to differ from you on certain equivocal points in your critique of my play this morning.' And if Lord Aberdare were to clout a ball high and hard, using Tyldesley's comically crossbat, it would be equally false — as though he were to say to me: 'Tha'rt a nice soart to talk about t'game. Ah'd like to bowl at thee!'

But of course, the truth about the English and cricket is much simpler than anything I have quoted so far. Hubert Phillips got it just right when he said:

An Englishman's crease is 'is castle.

CHAPTER THREE

Average Mongering and Money Making

Let us not have the notion that cricket was played for nothing
more than enjoyment during those early days. Here is a report
from the *Morning Herald* of 1807: when you see that 1000 guineas
were riding on the outcome, then the intensity of the game is
understood. (Note also the part played by John Willes, and his
new type of bowling.)

On Monday, July 20th, the return grand match between a
thirteen of All England and twenty-three of Kent, for one
thousand guineas, on Bennenden Heath, terminated in
favour of Kent by 162 runs. This was reckoned the greatest
match played in Kent for upwards of twenty years. Bets to a
large amount depended on both sides. The straight-arm
bowling, introduced by John Willes, Esq., was generally
practised in the game, and proved a great obstacle against
getting runs in comparison to what might have been got by
straightforward bowling. This bowling met with great
opposition. Mr. Willes and his bowling were frequently
barred in making a match, and he played sometimes amid
much uproar and confusion. Still he would persevere, till
the 'ring' closed on the players, the stumps were lawlessly
pulled up, and all came to a standstill.

During the 1790s, there are many records of matches played
for similar sums. Frederick Gale, writing in 1830, suggests that
sometimes, however, the leading figures of the time did not
always pay up:

Bowyer told me . . . how, in a match, when a noble lord
drew himself in the guinea lottery for runs, and was in with

him (Bowyer), he would not run any runs hardly but his own if he could help it, in order to get the lottery, and, said old Bowyer, 'Lord Ponsonby, who had drawn my name, promised me two guineas if I got most runs; but Lord _____ went backwards and forwards to the scorers to count his notches and mine, and the end of it was that he got 64 and I only got 60. Though,' said the old man, 'he did give me a guinea, Lord Ponsonby would have given me two, and I call that kind of thing which Lord _____ did "cheating" and nothing more or less.'

The early nineteenth-century diarist, Frederick Reynolds notes that members of the Marylebone Club were much given to practical jokes and appeared to bet on every aspect of the game.

Women too tested the fortunes of the cricketing gamblers. A three-day match held at Newington in 1811, played between two female teams was matched at 500 guineas a side.

Even the Laws of cricket were precise about Betting. Here is an extract from the Laws published in 1820:

BETS

If the Notches of one Player are laid against another, the Bets depend on the First Innings, unless otherwise specified.

If the Bets are made upon both Innings, and one Party beats the other in One Innings, the Notches in the First Innings shall determine the Bet.

But if the other Party goes in a second time, then the Bet must be determined by the number on the Score.

A. G. Steel, writing in the 1880s, dismissed the idea that betting had a grip on cricket, but he was none too pleased about the commercial way in which the game was going; Steel has a wonderfully pompous, reactionary style. Some might recognise the Steels of this world in their county committee rooms:

. . . I allude to the betting and book-making element which from the earliest days has been the curse of sport. What is the worst feature about horse-racing? To what do English

34

lovers of true sport owe the fact that every racecourse is the rendezvous of the biggest blackguards and knaves in the kingdom? Is it not betting, and the pecuniary inducement it offers to every kind of dirty, shabby practice? The sullying influence has spread to the running-path, and even, if report says true, to the river. Happily there is never the slightest whisper of suspicion against the straightness of our cricket players, and this is entirely owing to the absence of the betting element in connection with the game. It is an unfortunate fact that the tendency of first class cricket nowadays is to swamp the amateur by the professional. Some of our best county teams are almost wholly composed of the latter class . . . what has happened in consequence? Cricket — i.e. first-class cricket — is becoming a regular monetary speculation. Thousands upon thousands troop almost daily to see the big matches, flooding the coffers of county or club, which does its very best to spin out the match for the sake of the money. If this continues, our best matches will become nothing better than gate-money contests, to the detriment of the true interests of the game and its lovers.

During the Victorian period the fashion for open gambling does seem to have waned. However, for those who would see the financial inducements and sponsorship as a distasteful characteristic of the modern game, here is a reminder that nothing is new under the cricketing sun: it is a letter from W. G.'s brother, E. M. Grace in 1874, used in an advertisement by the batmaker Edward Page:

Dear Pulling,
I find there is still one bat due to me. Will you kindly get E. J. Page to make one for me half an inch longer than usual in the handle and 2lb 3oz in weight, and plenty of wood; tell him the last I had of his made over 6,000 runs and he is sure then to make me a good one. If he makes it now I can oil it all the winter.

Edward Mills Grace, Secretary Gloucs CCC

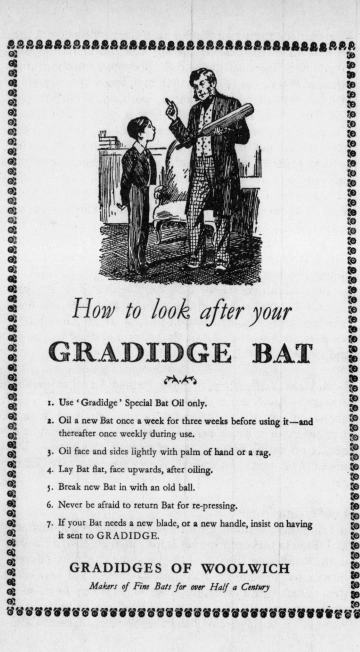

How to look after your
GRADIDGE BAT

꧁·ᴧ·꧂

1. Use 'Gradidge' Special Bat Oil only.

2. Oil a new Bat once a week for three weeks before using it—and thereafter once weekly during use.

3. Oil face and sides lightly with palm of hand or a rag.

4. Lay Bat flat, face upwards, after oiling.

5. Break new Bat in with an old ball.

6. Never be afraid to return Bat for re-pressing.

7. If your Bat needs a new blade, or a new handle, insist on having it sent to GRADIDGE.

GRADIDGES OF WOOLWICH
Makers of Fine Bats for over Half a Century

That sort of endorsement could not be bettered today. And for those who might complain that today's game is too commercialised, take comfort that the same sentiment was being expressed at the end of the nineteenth century, by none other than W. G. Grace:

I sometimes think that the modern conditions of cricket are too luxurious. County cricket is made too much of a business, and some of the best elements of the game have consequently been eliminated.

And, A. E. Knight the Leicestershire and England batsman wrote in 1906:

The modern cricket world is given over to average mongering and money making.

The Complete Cricketer

Average mongering and money making indeed! If that reads like a paragraph from some 1980s sporting leader column, then how about the following letter from *The Times* of 6 September 1909? A forerunner to the modern debate over imported players and the motives of the clubs that sign them up, it is about the Australian batsman Warren Bardsley:

The unfounded rumour that Mr. Bardsley was going to qualify for an English county has brought out a protest . . . against the whole system of the importation of colonial players. Middlesex have been the worst offenders, and their position of late years has been largely due to Trott and Tarrant. It is hoped that cases like these and that of Marshal, the Surrey player will not be repeated. If an amateur like Mr. Smith, of Northamptonshire, chooses to come and reside in England, and qualify for a county it is a different matter, provided that he plays as and is a bona fide amateur, although even this is not altogether to be encouraged; but when a professional does so it is only a flagrant instance of commercialism in cricket, and the present dispute in the football world shows what a deplorable state of things may prevail in this respect . . .

CHAPTER FOUR

At Thomas Lord's

Cricket has often been described as a game mainly for 'Southron folk', not least by Francis Thompson:

At Lord's

It is little I repair to the matches of the Southron folk,
Though my own red roses there may blow;
It is little that I repair to the matches of the Southron folk,
Though the red roses crest the caps, I know;
For the field is full of shades as I near the shadowy coast,
And a ghostly batsman plays to the bowling of a ghost,
And I look through my tears on a soundless-clapping host,
As the run-stealers flicker to and fro,
To and fro;
Oh my Hornby and my Barlow long ago!

Hornby and Barlow were long ago indeed, ancients of Lancashire and far from the southern domination of the M.C.C. and its Law makers. Yet Thomas Lord, who gave his name to the famous ground, was born in Yorkshire, at Thirsk in 1755. By all accounts he was a quick, underarm bowler. He made his fortune in London, in the wine business and had a public house in the Marylebone Road. This is not the place for a history of Lord's, yet it is worth reminding ourselves that today's Lord's is not the original, but the third ground. The first ground appeared in 1781 and was in the area of what is today, Balcombe Street, not far from Marylebone Road. In 1811, the ground was moved to a site between Grove Road and Park Road. Then in 1814, the present ground was established in St John's Wood.

In *The Times*'s *History of the M.C.C.*, it is recorded that the

Marylebone Club played its first match on Lord's ground in May 1788, a year after the founding of the M.C.C.:

At that time the ground was described as being in the country — it was very little more than an open field, though by 1793 it had been surrounded by a wooden paling and a small wooden shed served the purpose of a pavilion. This venture was a complete success, and by 1800 it was not unusual for a crowd of 4,000 to 5,000 spectators to pay 6d. for admission to watch the matches. These numbers were no doubt attracted to a large extent by the very important part played by gambling in the game of that period . . .

. . . Lord allowed his ground to be used for many other purposes than that of cricket. For instance, it was the scene of many athletic, pigeon shooting, and hopping matches, and even on one occasion of a balloon ascent . . .

The history of the Lord's ground is dotted with financial problems as well as scenes of cricketing feats. What is more, the headquarters of cricket has had its share of fireworks, and not always in the cricketing sense as the *Morning Post* of 7 May 1814 reported:

A shocking accident occurred on Thursday at the New Lord's Cricket ground public house, Mary-le-bone fields. The landlady of the house had occasion to use a small quantity of gunpowder, and whilst in the act of taking the same from a paper, containing a pound weight, a spark from the fire caught it and it went off with a great explosion. The landlady, her sister, and two little girls who were in the room were seriously burnt. The two former are in a dangerous way. The explosion broke every pane of glass in the room and also set it on fire.

And the same paper in 1825 reported:

DESTRUCTION OF THE ASSEMBLY, BETTING AND
DRESSING ROOMS AT LORD'S CRICKET GROUNDS

About one o'clock yesterday morning a fire was discovered

in the above ornamental buildings, attached to the far-famed grounds belonging formerly to Mr. Lord (but now in the possession of a Mr. Ward), in which, perhaps, some of the greatest cricketers have played and alternatively won and lost thousands . . . Our reporter, who was on the spot, endeavoured by every means to find out by what accident the fire had taken place, but all he could learn was, that a party had been in the ground in the afternoon, and after their departure the rooms had been left in supposed security.

Morning Post, 30 July 1825.

It will come as no surprise to learn that in the early days, Lord's was far from the smooth, great ground of the present. Remember, the grounds, including the first one, were in the countryside surrounding London. One superb description of the scenes at St John's Wood was given by Sir Spencer Ponsonby-Fane, a founder member in 1845 of the famous wandering side I Zingari. In his memoirs, Sir Spencer wrote:

. . . there was the public house, a long, low building on the south side, separated from the ground by a row of clipped lime-trees, and a few green benches on which the thirsty spectators smoked long pipes and enjoyed drinks. Round the ground there were more of these small benches without backs, and a pot-boy walked round with a supply of beer and porter for the public, who had no other means of refreshing themselves. Excepting these benches there were no seats for spectators. At the south-east corner of the ground there were large stacks of willow-blocks to be seasoned and made into bats in the workshop adjoining. On the upper north-east corner was a large sheep-pen . . .

And elsewhere he wrote:

In the centre of the ground, opposite the Pavilion, was a square patch of grass kept constantly rolled and taken care of. No scythe was allowed to touch it . . . the rest of the ground was ridge and furrow . . . on non-match days the public could have a pitch for a shilling which included the use of stumps, bat and ball . . . The grass was never mowed.

40

THE GRAPHIC

AN ILLUSTRATED WEEKLY NEWSPAPER

SATURDAY, JULY 19, 1884

WITH EXTRA SUPPLEMENT

PRICE SIXPENCE
By Post Sixpence Half

The Eton-Harrow match at Lord's of 1884 attracted a not-too-serious illustrated report in The Graphic. *As ever, it was a great social occasion*

It was usually kept down by a flock of sheep which was penned up on match days, and on Saturdays four or five hundred sheep were driven on to the ground on their way to the Monday Smithfield Market . . . half a dozen boys picked out the rough stalks of grass . . .

More than one hundred years later, here is T. C. Dodds, of Essex, writing in *Hit Hard and Enjoy It*, summing up the perfect combination — Lord's and a Test match:

For cricket-lovers there is no place quite like Lord's during a Test match. Lord's must be a bit like Heaven. There are many mansions in it. It caters for all tastes, classes, colours, ages, points of view, degrees of skill, levels of knowledge.

CHAPTER FIVE

The Old Man

Lord's may have seen more degrees of skill and heard levels of knowledge expressed (especially from The Tavern) than any other ground. However it would be almost impossible to know for certain which player had the greatest skill. Because The Game is ever changing and possibly because we have no visual record of the early players, mercifully there is no way of knowing who was the greatest. One of the joys of any sport is the seemingly never ending debate about the style, technique and ability of one player compared with a thousand others. But if it were possible to get all the great batsmen of the past together at Lord's, I wonder which one would give the true masterclass? To say 'I was coached by Bradman or Hutton, or Hobbs or Gunn, or Hammond, or Hendren, or Ranji,' or any of the others with names one associates with genius, would allow one to dine out for months of a season. As a schoolboy, I was always Compton, but if I were to be allowed one fantasy, it would have to be a meeting with W. G. Grace.

'Excuse me Sir, but I seem to have this problem with my off-drive . . .'

Well, for those who have often wondered how the Old Man went about his batting, here is an extract from his *Reminiscences*. He starts by telling us (and this was more than eighty years ago remember) that there is not much to be gained from this modern idea of the batsman taking guard like some imported baseball player.

Do not get into the irritating habit of flourishing your bat in the air. Nothing is gained by it, and sometimes a good deal is lost by it.

Personally, I find that the greatest scope for freedom of

play is secured by holding the bat in what is called the pendulum fashion, which tends to facility of movement, without diminishing in the slightest degree that batsman's power of defence.

I await the attack of the bowler with the top of the handle of my bat just above my waist, and the bottom of the blade almost on a level with the centre of the middle stump . . .

Confidence comes with experience, and until confidence is acquired a batsman's defence cannot be good. An uncertain and vacillating style spells failure, for in batting he who hesitates is assuredly lost. So make up your mind how you intend playing a ball, and then play it confidently and resolutely, hitting hard if you are going to hit, and blocking vigorously if you intend to block. Do not allow the bat to passively await the impact of the ball.

And Grace's earliest memories of his own learning, paints also a picture of times past:

I learned the rudiments of cricket when quite a child. As small boys we played about the garden in a rough and ready way, and used to make the nurses bowl to us.

A new meaning for the Nursery End? Grace may have been a natural ball player, but he once wrote that natural ability is not enough:

I should like to say that good batsmen are born, not made; but my long experience comes up before me, and tells me that it is not so.

Cricket, 1891

Not every one reveres the memory of the Old Man's performance however; here's a verse from Oscar Lloyd's 'Grace at Gloucester':

I saw the 'Old Man' once
When he was old as I
Was young. He did not score,
So far as I recall, a heap of runs,
Nor even hit a four.

Most pictures of Grace show him with a bat in his hand and it is sometimes forgotten that he was a very fine bowler as well as a supreme batsman. During his first class career, W. G. took 2,864 wickets at an average of 17.97 apiece. His batting average in 1,389 completed innings was 39.53 with a total of 54,904 runs and a top score of 344 in 1876 for M.C.C. against Kent at Canterbury.

Grace took his bowling seriously — as did the many batsmen who faced him. However, Grace was a somewhat strong-willed character who tended to like, and often get, his own way. On one occasion it is said that he had been bowling for some considerable time and his captain, a little apprehensively suggested a change. W. G. agreed immediately. 'I'll go on at the other end,' he said. And did!

Of course, he did hit many a four, and filled more lines in the scorebooks than did most of his time. Incidentally, the first scoreboard that showed a batsman's runs as they came, was appropriately erected at Lord's, and, inevitably, the first man to have runs registered on the new board, was W. G. Grace. He would have considered it only proper.

Grace came from a cricketing family and there are those historians of The Game who say that Grace's brother, E. M. was as good. He is one of only four people ever to have taken ten wickets and scored a century in the same innings. (Inevitably, his brother did it also!) E. M. Grace's double was at Canterbury, and this inscription on the base of the match ball, says it all:

With this ball
(presented by M.C.C. to E. M. GRACE),
he got every wicket in 2nd innings, in the
match played at Canterbury,
AUGUST 14, 15, 1862,
GENTLEMEN OF KENT v. M.C.C.,
for whom he played as an emergency, and
in which, going in first,
he scored
192 NOT OUT.

W. G. Grace was as agile on his after-dinner feet as he was at the wicket — from either end. R. A. Fitzgerald remembers that during the 1872 tour of Canada, Grace was called upon to make a number of speeches of thanks. The first was delivered in Montreal. There followed a number of thank-yous — all with a familiar ring. First, Montreal:

Gentlemen, I beg to thank you for the honour you have done me. I never saw better bowling than I have seen to-day, and I hope to see as good wherever I go.

The team went on to Ottawa, where W. G.'s speech was similar to the one delivered in Montreal:

Gentlemen, I beg to thank you for the honour you have done me. I never saw a better ground than I have seen today, and I hope to see as good wherever I go.

And so on to Toronto and another long night of speech writing, which produced:

Gentlemen, I thank you for the honour you have done me. I have never seen better batting than I saw today, and I hope to see as good wherever I go.

And at another dinner in the same city:

Gentlemen, I have to thank you for the honour you have done me. I have never met such good fellows as I met today, and I hope I shall meet as good wherever I go.

Finally in Hamilton:

Gentlemen, I have to thank you for the honour you have done me. I have never seen prettier ladies than I have seen today, and I hope I shall see as pretty wherever I go.

Well not *quite* finally; the team went on to America. Soon after arriving in New York, W. G. was called upon to speak. Never a man to be stuck for words, especially the same ones . . .

Gentlemen, I have to thank you for the honour you have done me. I have never tasted better oysters than I have tasted here today, and I hope I shall get as good wherever I go.

On other subjects Grace was more forthcoming, not least on women cricketers. Female cricket is not a modern phenomenon. An engraving dating from 1770 entitled, Miss Wicket, shows a young lady in a rather casual pose and fine clothes, including a most elaborate hat, standing with curved bat before two stumps. And in 1811 a splendid etching by Thomas Rowlandson is called, a Cricket Match Extraordinary. It took place, somewhat late in the season, October, although the two sides appear dressed for fine weather. The year was 1811 and the scene was at Ball's Pond, Middlesex, where eleven ladies of Surrey and eleven of Hampshire played for 500 guineas a side. James Laver's *English Sporting Prints*, records that, 'The demon bowler, on this occasion, was an

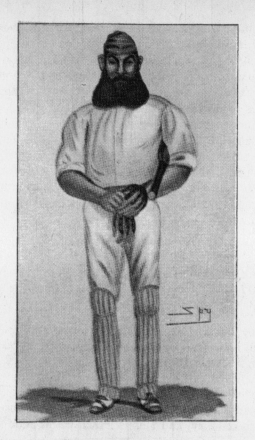

W. G. Grace, 1877

old lady of sixty, and it is astonishing to learn that she wore "loose trousers, with short fringed petticoats descending to the knees".'

Eighty years later, the casual game of cricket between ladies had given way to more organised sides. Commenting on the sight of skirt-wearing teams during the 1891 season, W. G. Grace made it very clear that in his mind, lady cricketers should be declared B.N.G. — Batspersons non grata:

A new chapter — and a short one — was added to the annals of cricket by the appearance this season of two Elevens of

'Lady Cricketers', who travelled about the country and played exhibition matches. They claimed that they did play, and not burlesque, the game, but interest in their doings did not survive long. Cricket is not a game for women, and although the fair sex occasionally join in a picnic game, they are not constitutionally adapted for the sport. If the lady cricketers expected to popularise the game among women they failed dismally. At all events, they had their day and ceased to be.

Clearly, a woman's place is in the tea-hut.

Today, women cricketers are welcomed and encouraged, although in the hallowed halls of the cricket establishment, there are clearly reservations about how long is arms length. Take this delightful reminder that cricket has not succumbed to batspersons: it is from the 1985 *Wisden*. Netta Rheinberg is writing in the section on 'Women's Cricket, 1984', commenting on Surrey's Janette Brittin,

> She used her feet well and despatched the ball elegantly to all quarters of the field, bringing back memories of a former outstanding England batsman, Molly Hide.

A fine batsman indeed; also, neither Hide nor Brittin is mentioned in *Wisden*'s index. Women cricketers appear not to worry too much about being tagged as men. Probably they are of the same sound breed of women for whom the title Madam Chairman is recognition enough. This acceptance of the lady's lot stretches to the sometimes outspoken Sarah Potter. A very handy Hereford and sometimes England cricketer, she has some very straight views about women and cricket:

> People laugh and jeer at what they think is a bunch of big strapping hairy-lipped girls but I feel we have as much right to play cricket as any beer-swilling bloke, half drunk, with a bulging pot-belly. We all play for the same reason, which is enjoyment of the game. It makes us happy . . .
> I have people in my club who are hopeless, absolutely

hopeless, but they want to get away from their husbands and the kids cooking Sunday lunch, and I don't see why they shouldn't.

And if to emphasise that in cricket there's no need for batspersons:

I love the physical side of fast bowling and I love being a *batsman*.

CHAPTER SIX

Ex-Gentlemen and Players

This image of the bulging-bellied batsman, bowler or even wicket keeper, is almost entirely confined to village, or local cricket. The great county and international heroes of The Game have generally kept an image of trimness, leaving the more burly and brawling reputation for, say, the rugby fraternity. Until recent years, however, cricket had a reputation for being a game that required almost no degree of sporting fitness unless you happened to be a bowler. Possibly the civilized image has had something to do with cream or white clothing, summer sun and the need to come in out of the rain so often. At one time, the image was neatly divided between the amateurs and the professionals, the Gentlemen and Players.

In the days of Gentlemen and Players, the professional was often portrayed as the antithesis of the cashmere-bred amateur. The professional was raw-boned, drank his beer from a straight glass and accepted his bonus with a silent touch of his short back and sides. Edgar Oldroyd died shortly after Christmas 1964, yet he had started his cricket in the nineteenth century. It matters not whether he was a Gentleman or a Player, his tough Yorkshire outline illustrated the professional image of that county's cricket. Who better to capture it than R. C. Robertson-Glasgow:

His name might have been Jess Oakroyd. I'm not sure that it oughtn't to have been. For, as a cricketer, he was a type rather than an individual. He was one of those small, tough, humorous, militant men who make the comedy and the greatness of a country. They are to be found answering back something or somebody which may or may not have existence: fate, a tax-collector, Monday morning, a bus-conductor, thirst, or a Hyde Park orator. They bounce and

51

argue down time's corridors. And they generally win the battle.

Oldroyd could not be one of those who, when they are abruptly bowled by a snorter, accept the unwelcome visitation with a resigned calm. He was very angry indeed; and he looked it, and often said it. For you had not only ended Oldroyd for some hours; you'd ended an integral section of Yorkshire. You'd wrecked a parish and interfered with the workings of the only country that mattered. And there lies the secret of the Yorkshire cricketer. He comes second in his own estimation; and he despises, if silently, those who cannot play to this philosophy.

R. C. Robertson-Glasgow's observations of his fellow cricketers and those who followed him remain a joy. Here he is remembering his Somerset colleague M. D. Lyon, who although younger than Oldroyd, died in the same year, 1964.

Lyon's wicket-keeping varied from the brilliant to the blandly inattentive. He objected to wide inswingers on the leg side, and, as the ball sped to the flower-border in front of the Taunton pavilion, he would remark casually: 'Tut, tut; there go four more gerania.'

It is said that Lyon's sometimes sharp wit kept him out of the England side of the 1920s. But if the selectors were aware of Lyon's tongue, it is by no means certain that they could always put a name to a wit. Robertson-Glasgow remembers having a long chat with Lord Harris:

He asked me many things about Somerset cricket, and wondered why I was not batting higher that day. I said, by way of a joke, that I always wondered that. Two wickets fell, and I excused myself. 'Well,' he said, 'goodbye Lyon; it's been nice to have a chat . . .'

I suppose the former England captain and Kent leader could not be expected to know everybody. However, one has had the impression that Robertson-Glasgow did know everybody. Certainly his series of pen portraits bring out the characters of even the most enigmatic players. Sometimes it is nothing more than a simple sentence to remind the reader of a very special cricketer and, a very special writer. To start with, here he is writing about Bob Wyatt, who in 1934 followed Douglas Jardine as England captain, played for both Warwickshire and Worcestershire and during the 1926-27 M.C.C. tour of Ceylon, took 5 for 39 (including a hat-trick) and scored a century in the same game:

His bat is as the crook to the shepherd, as the mace to the sergeant-at-arms. I would not doubt that his first cry from the cradle was an appeal for l.b.w.

And on Harold Larwood:

Once, in a County match, when Larwood was in the middle of that glorious run-up, the batsman raised his hand and stopped him. Perhaps the dull reason was simply that he

wasn't ready. I think, rather, that the batsman, a humble enough performer, was seized with that last love of life which must have urged victims of old to address some trivial and delaying remark to the executioner. A few seconds later the blow fell, and the bails whizzed past the wicket-keeper.

Both Larwood and Wyatt played in the infamous 1932-3 tour of Australia. The Australian captain, Bill Woodfull was by all accounts a steadfast character, not unlike the bedrock of recent Australian cricket, Alan Border. Woodfull, Robertson-Glasgow wrote:

. . . had the gaze of a mariner and the mind of a master who gets the whole school to and from a Bank-holiday picnic without losing his reason or a boy.

And on another famous Australian of the same period:

Bill O'Reilly was a fighter. He looked as if, under necessary circumstance, he might have founded or sacked a city. It was a face and form such as you might have seen in a picture of explorers or pioneers. At cricket he would have bowled till his boots burst, and after. If only one cricket ball was left in the world, and that one came to pieces in his hand, he would whizz down a leg-break with the largest fragment.

Robertson-Glasgow's picture of Patsy Hendren who, in 1935 and at the age of forty-six, was still playing for England, starts with a shake of the head at cricket itself:

Cricket, sometimes a rather solemn and calculating old bloke, will never forget Elias ('Patsy') Hendren. He played around cricket, and pulled at it, and called it names, and provoked it, and loved it. When he stopped playing for Middlesex, cricket must have missed its imp, its laughing familiar, as Lord's missed its hero. Hendren has been called a clown; but he was more like the 'Fool' who called Lear 'nuncy' and tried to keep the old man from going mad by a stream of talk that poured unmixed from the elemental humours of the earth.

One of the more flamboyant figures of 1930s cricket was P. G. H. Fender. 'Percy George' played for both Sussex and Surrey. It was for Surrey that Fender scored the fastest ever hundred, in 35 minutes. 'Percy George' died in June 1985 and Frank Keating, writing in *The Guardian* wrote:

His friend Robertson-Glasgow, breeziest and best of all cricket essayists, once said that nobody could match Fender's capacity for sheer entertainment in everything he did.

He hated a dull finish, the formal declaration, the expected stroke, the workaday over. He rescued treasures of cricket from dust and oblivion, snatched off the covering, and showed them to an astonished and delighted public. He would declare an innings closed with an abruptness which threatened committee men with heart failure . . .

Having declared myself as a devoted fan of Compton, who might well have been called the breeziest of players on occasions, here is the breeziest and best of all cricket essayists on my hero:

The first time that I saw Denis Compton was in the nets at Lord's. He was bowling slow left-hand to an elderly member who wore a wildly improbable cap. Both performers were in a state of amusement and heat. Exercise rather than practice was being obtained . . . there was an abandon about the scene that cannot be forgotten; a copious enjoyment . . . Enjoyment, given and felt, is the chief thing about Compton's batting. It has an ease and freshness which the formality of the first-class game has not injured. It is a clear flowing stream; a breath of half-holidays among work-days . . . nature and environment have been very good to him. Set fair to greatness.

That was written towards the end of the War, perhaps four years before that glorious 1947 season and those 18 centuries.

As a reminder that not all fine cricket writing ceased in the 1940s, here is *The Guardian*'s Frank Keating in 1984, after Bob Willis had announced his retirement. In just a few lines, Keating captures the essence of Willis's character, his style and his devastating power as a bowler perfectly. And as a bonus, tells us a story that few of us had heard.

So the beaky old bird they all call The Goose is grounding himself for good. Enjoy for one last summer the staring beady eyes and the gallop up the runway — arms, knees, elbows and elastic bandages, flapping this way and that in the effort to get airborne . . . Now, for his gravestone, we can metaphorically give the order to the mason — 'Headingley '81 — 8 for 43.' . . . After it finished and the Ashes were won, Bob drove that afternoon back to Birmingham. He switched on the car radio. It said England had won and Willis had taken 8 for 43. Not till that moment had it sunk in. Bob had to pull into the hard shoulder, have a lie down and a pleasant little trance.

And, of modern cricket writers, who could pass by John

Woodcock. In this single sentence he captures the complete image of one of the most delightful, but at the same time, infuriating cricketers of the past twenty years, Geoffrey Boycott:

> Boycott's idea of bliss might be to bat all night (so long as it was not for Mr Packer) having batted all day . . .

One of the joys of Woodcock's writing is his use of understatement. When there must be a temptation to burst into glowing or angry print, he somehow makes his point in what might be called an old fashioned way. Here is a passage, written *before* the much discussed 1986 winter tour of the West Indies by the England side; Woodcock is writing as Editor of the 1985 *Wisden* — the subject is short pitched bowling:

> It was hard to watch the West Indian, Marshall, bowling at Pocock in last season's fifth Test match at The Oval without recoiling. Pocock was the night-watchman from the previous day. As such, he could expect few favours. However, the Laws of Cricket make it abundantly clear that the 'relative skills of the striker' must be taken into consideration by an umpire when deciding whether the bowling of fast, short-pitched balls amounts to 'intimidation' and is therefore unfair. That Marshall, a superb bowler, should have kept bouncing the ball at so an inept a batsman as Pocock was unwarrantable; that Lloyd should have condoned his doing so was disconcerting; that Constant, the umpire at Marshall's end should have stood passively by was unaccountable. It was a woeful piece of cricket entirely lacking in chivalry.

In spite of bodyline (Ancient & Modern), cricket has managed to retain an image of being a game of chivalry. Possibly this is largely to do with the image of those at the forefront of The Game during the past hundred years. Also, the way in which cricket has been reported has tended to reflect the thought that The Game is really full of schoolboy enthusiasm. That enthusiasm matched with a sense of days gone by, is charmingly set out in the late Pelham Warner's history of Lord's, called simply, *Lord's 1787-1945*. This superb example of simple cricket reporting comes from the latter period. It is full of understatement and the type of phrasing that has not changed in more than forty years. Warner is writing during the period which he called The Second German War. There was, in 1945, a series of unofficial Tests against Australia. The Australians had done rather well:

> In the third match at Lord's on July 14, 16 and 17, Australia won again, by four wickets, though England was dogged by misfortune. Hutton scored 104 and 69, and held the side together in the first innings in a total of 254. Places were given to the Etonian the Hon. L. R. White, the Reptonian D. B. Carr, and J. G. Dewes, who had made over 1000 runs for Cambridge. None of these quite realised expectations, though Dewes batted soundly for 27 in England's first innings.
> Australia were dismissed for 194, Pollard having a fine analysis of six for 75. The England side had to take to the field after the first day without Hammond, who was seized with lumbago and took no further part in the match, while Washbrook, because of a badly damaged thumb, went in very late in the second innings, and batted practically with one hand.
> The Australians were left to make 225, and though they won, had Miller been caught at deep square leg with his score at 38, victory might have rested with the England side.

The very idea of Hammond being 'seized with lumbago'! Imagine the reasons for not playing today — lumbago would hardly figure in the first ten of fashionable injuries. Incidentally, this was the end of the 'Second German War' and here is Warner mentioning the arrival of not a cricketing hero, but a war hero Montgomery. (Although he did come from a cricketing family.)

> Field-Marshal Montgomery was at Lord's for a few hours one afternoon. As his car entered the Members' Gate he was cheered to the echo, the pavilion standing up to welcome him.

Imagine in one afternoon, Hammond (watching), Hutton, Miller, Edrich, Washbrook and Montgomery: heroes all, the very stuff of schoolboy dreams. If I had a schoolboy hero, other than Compton, it must have been Teddy Lester. Lester was the invention of John Finnemore in the 1920s. Finnemore wrote books for real boys which had titles such as *A Boy Scout with the Russians, A Boy Scout in the Balkans, The Outlaw of the Shell* and most importantly for me, *Teddy Lester's Schooldays*. Lester was at Slapton School, and I seem to remember that when I was about five or six I announced that I too wanted to go on to Slapton when I was thirteen so that I could play cricket with Lester. My mother had the difficult task of explaining that Slapton and Lester were fictional. She might just as well have said that Father Christmas was not true — I could not think anything but that she was surely wrong.

My favourite book, was *Teddy Lester, Captain of Cricket*. In true 1920s style, although Lester is the hero, Finnemore realised that the main character could not be stretched to bat, bowl, field and keep wicket better than every other boy at Slapton. The school is playing Hazlemere and the hero for Slapton is young Frank Sandys. Note how the language is a mixture of Richard Hannay, Bulldog Drummond and Greyfriars. Slapton is batting with Teddy Lester at one end and the young Frank Sandys at the other. Lester is in absolute control . . . or is he?

Off the first ball of the next over Teddy made a pretty late cut for three, and Frank went up to the batting wicket. The next three balls from the slow man were very good, and there wasn't the ghost of a chance to get one away.

Then, as slow men sometimes will, he overpitched one, and Frank charged at it with all the force of his powerful little shoulders. But a most dreadful catastrophe happened.

'Come on,' shouted Teddy, for there was a single, if no more. The ball had been driven towards long-off, who was far too deep to save the run. The bowler had darted at great speed to place himself upon the path, but he could not save the single and every run was useful.

But this is what happened — an accident in a thousand. The bowler missed fielding the ball, and it hit him a frightful crack on the shin and was turned aside. It bounded straight into the wicket which Teddy had just left, and a bail fell . . .

Slapton looked uneasy. Teddy Lester gone! He took a full half of their hopes with him as he retreated to the pavilion.

All now rests on Sandys, 'the young un' as Finnemore has Lester calling him. Other batsmen come in, other batsmen go. The contest is between Frank Sandys and the mighty and feared Hazlemere bowler, Kerrison. Four to win! The tension is tremendous. Every eye is glued on the pitch, and every Slapton heart is longing to see the fine little bat whip one to the boundary, and thus make the winning hit.

But the bowler is doing his utmost, and his utmost is very good. Frank dares not hit. There is no ball which, either in length or in direction is hittable. And so it comes to the last ball of the over.

As the bowler begins to run the silence is profound. If this ball produced no runs then Kerrison would be let loose upon the unlucky last man, and it was a million to one that Hazlemere would snatch a victory at the last moment.

Crack! There was a roar from Slapton throats . . . then the cry was checked, as they saw a fieldsman come tearing across, field the ball splendidly, and return it like lightning.

Frank was leisurely trotting down the pitch . . . he had got the batting at any rate.

Kerrison then runs in to bowl to Sandys . . .

But Frank was ready for it. Rising to the whole of his very modest height, he got over it, and brought his bat down with a terrific slash.

How all Slapton rose to that tremendous last smite! The winning hit! Victory after all! . . . One shout of Sandys! Sandys! filled the air, and a rush was made for the little scurrying figure . . . they pounced on him half-way and swung him up and carried him in triumph. Then upon the very steps of the pavilion there was a striking scene.

On the top step stood Teddy Lester, captain of cricket, his eyes shining with delight for the fine victory which his little new recruit had gained. And as the procession marched up the steps, carrying Frank Sandys on high, Teddy stepped forward, took his own First Eleven cap from his head, and placed it on Frank's bare head, thus giving him the coveted dignity of a First Eleven cap in public, and with the greatest honour possible.

Frank Sandys being carried on high

Montgomery cheered through the Members' Gate twenty odd
years later, would have loved the hero and admired the dramatic
gesture of Lester — a Field-Marshal's baton in every cricket bag.

61

CHAPTER SEVEN

Most Abuse and Least Thanks

Cricketing portraits too often deal only with cricketers. Not very much is written about those often anonymous stalwarts of The Game, the umpires. Yet, some of them have achieved enormous respect and, in spite of some of their decisions, affection. This, for example, is how Frank Chester was described by Diana Rait Kerr and Ian Peebles in *Lord's 1946-1970*:

> . . . for many years the keenness of his senses, his power of sustained concentration, and his professional knowledge made him a seemingly infallible judge of any cricket situation.

Chester was only sixty-two when he died in 1957. As a boy, I remember seeing him at the Oval and being surprised to be told that he had once played for Worcestershire. I was surprised because until then I had thought that umpires were made at Lord's. I thought also, that it looked an easy job!

It has never been that. A. G. Steel writing in the *Cricket* edition of the Badminton Library towards the end of the last century, put it this way:

> If anyone were to ask us the question 'What class of useful men receive most abuse and least thanks for their service?' we should, without hesitation, reply, 'Cricket umpires.' The duties of an umpire are most laborious and irksome; they require for their proper performance the exercise of numerous qualifications, and yet it is always the lot of every man who dons the white coat, the present dress of an umpire, to receive, certainly no thanks, and, too frequently, something which is not altogether unlike abuse.

And Steel remembers a village match in Hampshire, probably in the 1870s, maybe a few years earlier:

The village umpire there, a jolly, good-natured old man, but absolutely ignorant of the laws of cricket, caused us the greatest merriment during the whole day. In addition to his official post as umpire, he was the village caterer at all public entertainments, and consequently supplied luncheon at all the matches. It was evident his thoughts in the field were divided between the responsibilities of his two duties — at least we inferred so by his occasionally allowing the bowler to bowl as much as ten or more balls an over, and giving as his reason, 'If Mr. — doant have a bot o' exercise, he won't relish my steak pie. O'im vaamous for steak pies, yer know, sir,' he added by way of apology for introducing the subject.

When Steel was playing in Scotland, he was batting with a baronet at the other end. The landed batsman was surviving an enormous number of very reasonable appeals for l.b.w. and catches at the wicket. Steel records:

. . . the writer ventured humbly to ask the umpire whether the last appeal (an enormous thigh right in front of all three stumps to a straight one) had not been a very near thing. 'Lor bless you sir,' was the reply, 'I have been his valet for fifteen years, and I dussn't give him out; he gets awful wild at times.'

Umpiring developed from the notcher. He was the fellow who sat close by and simply notched the score up on a piece of wood. In the eighteenth century it was decided that umpires were not only necessary, they needed a set of Laws (not rules, but Laws) to give them authority.

Laws for ye Umpires

To allow 2 Minutes for each man to come in when one is out, and 10 Minutes between each Hand.

To mark ye Ball that it may not be changed.

They are sole judge of all Outs and Ins, of all fair and

unfair play, of frivolous delays, of all hurts, whether real or pretended, and are discretionally to allow what time they think proper before ye game goes on again.

In case of a real hurt to a Striker, they are to allow another to come in and ye Person hurt to come in again, but are not to allow a fresh Man to play, on either side, on any Account.

They are the sole judge of all hindrances, crossing ye Players in running, and standing unfair to strike, and in case of hindrance may order a Notch to be scored.

They are not to order any Man out unless appealed to by one of ye Players.

These laws are to ye Umpires jointly.

Each Umpire is ye sole judge of all Nips and Catches, Ins and Outs, good or bad Runs, at his own Wicket, and his determination shall be absolute, and he shall not be changed for another Umpire without ye consent of both Sides.

When ye 4 Balls are bowled, he is to call Over.

These Laws are separately.

When both Unpires shall call Play, 3 times, 'tis at ye peril of giving ye Game from them that refuse to play.

Of course, a set of Laws did not resolve problems, nor did the written directions remove the wonderful individuality from the wooden-faced judges. Lord Harris' favourite story was about a nineteenth-century bowler-turned-umpire called Henry Royston. Royston is said to have given a famous batsman as run out, even though the man was well in his crease. The cause apparently was that there wasn't much time left for the game and if the batsman had survived at the wicket for much longer, then the fielding side had no chance of winning. Royston did not think much of this situation and so gave the batsman out. 'We're obliged,' he said, 'to study them things, you know, else 'ow are we going to win our matches?'

It was a combination of uncertain, and sometimes timid, umpires, plus quite intimidating bowling and bowlers that produced the modern No Ball Law. So fierce was the bowler Jack Crossland, that the nineteenth-century umpires of the day

appeared to be afraid to call him for throwing. (The poor old umpire! If all else fails, blame the umpire.) At the time, umpires were not highly trained and they needed all the help they could get. By 1883, Lord Harris left things had got out of hand and announced that as umpires were reluctant to penalise bowlers then he, Harris, would propose new wording to the laws of cricket to force an umpire to call, 'No Ball!' when he was anything less than certain that the ball had been delivered fairly.

*

W. G. Grace's impression of the 1873 tour of Australia includes some caustic observations on umpiring:

About 7000 spectators were on the ground, and when we arrived they cheered enthusiastically.

As I was being shown round one of the players remarked, 'You see we manage our crowds better than you do in England. Our spectators are impartial and good-tempered. We never experience any unpleasantness on our cricket grounds.' Within a quarter of an hour this remark was refuted in a curious way. One of the umpires gave a decision displeasing to the batting side — which wanted just a few runs to win the cup — and a wrangle ensued, in the course of which the spectators broke into the ground. Ultimately the players left the field, abandoning the match in its unfinished condition. This, I am sorry to say, was a foretaste of some experiences which subsequently fell to our lot. It was a manifestation of the spirit which still unfortunately seems to survive in Australia, though not in so malignant a form as in the seventies.

Australia has always been deficient in the matter of good umpires, and though we in England are by no means perfect in this respect, the Australians are a long way behind us. In those days professional umpires were almost unheard of in Australia. Anyone who took an intelligent interest in cricket was thought good enough to umpire. Consequently inexperienced men had the delicate and onerous duty thrust upon them, with the result that no confidence was placed in their judgment and scant respect was paid to their decisions. I attribute the friction which has frequently arisen during the visits of English teams to Australia to the fact that even at the present time Australia is not well provided with good umpires.

★

Umpires then are remembered for their bad decisions and hints that they are human after all. Take the case of the badly fitting

teeth, recalled by one Charles Ponsonby in a letter he wrote to *The Times* on 12 August 1935:

Sir,
    I am glad that Mr. Aidan Crawley has called attention to the horrible suggestion made by Mr. F. G. J. Ford that alterations in the leg-before-wicket rule should apply to village cricket.
    Umpires in village cricket are all honourable men and try to temper their judgments with discretion, but they often suffer from defects both in training and physique. The majority of them have no training in the art of umpiring; some have never played cricket themselves, and many would frankly admit that they are unfit for cricket, too old, too fat,

or too slow. Some even have defective dental arrangements which interfere with a quick decision.

I was playing in a match last year and as the bowler delivered the ball the umpire ejaculated 'brrr', and after a pause, 'I beg your pardon, I meant to say no-ball, but I dropped my teeth.'

Of course not every village umpire suffers from defects. Some are very good and all do their best in this very difficult position.

Yours faithfully,
CHARLES PONSONBY

The South African cricket writer, Louis Duffus, had a fund of umpire stories. Here is one concerning Monty Noble, who captained Australia against P. F. Warner's M.C.C. side during the 1903-04 tour:

Monty Noble, the famous Australian captain, moved to glance at a ball very much on the leg side. He missed his stroke and the wicket-keeper, no doubt elated at smartly fielding a delivery difficult to take, appealed loudly. Much to Noble's chagrin he was given out. On the way back to the pavilion, as he passed the umpire, he asked, 'Where's your dog?'

The official was mystified by the remark, and when the teams came off the field sought out Noble for an explanation.

'You asked, Mr. Noble,' he said, 'how was my dog? I don't understand. I haven't got a dog.'

'Well,' said Noble, 'you're the first blind man I've ever seen without one.'

Jock Livingston, who played for New South Wales and Northants, tells of a very fierce game between his adopted English club and Yorkshire — in Yorkshire. Apparently, the tough Australian was, as usual, proving very difficult to get out and playing text-book head down and over the ball cricket. The large Yorkshire crowd were getting very fed up with this performance and even the wives had been instructed to put more coal in the grates to send black smoke across the ground. Livingston remained entrenched, when there was a very half-hearted appeal for l.b.w. from the bowler and nobody else, but which was then taken up by the spectators. To Livingston's astonishment, up went the umpire's finger. Later, Livingston, in that mild manner of his remarked to the umpire that the decision must have been close to say the least. The umpire agreed, 'Trouble is,' he said, 'I'd sooner upset one Australian than 10,000 bloody Yorkshiremen.'

Keith Miller has two of the best umpire tales, one about Alec Skelding the other about a Chinaman, Eric Lee Kow. Eric Lee Kow was standing in the 1955 series in the West Indies.

I made 140-odd in the Barbados Test in one innings, during the course of which I snicked a ball hard and was caught by the wicket-keeper. I turned and started to walk. As I went past Everton Weekes and Clyde Walcott they said, 'Hey, Keith, he hasn't given you out.' I turned and looked at the umpire and, to my astonishment, I saw him bending over the stumps removing them for the tea interval. It was obvious that he did not think I had hit it. I knew I was out however, and out I remained. The umpire, a Chinaman called Eric Lee Kow, met me at a cocktail party that evening and he referred to the incident.

'I didn't think you hit it . . . thank you for going.'

In the next innings Atkinson bowled a ball to me which turned back sharply from the off. I snicked it hard on to my pad. Atkinson uttered half an appeal, but, seeing me get a touch, he smothered his cry. Yet his half-shout was enough, for up went the umpire's finger and I was out — l.b.w. It was the same umpire!

And this is Miller on Alec Skelding:

The greatest character among the white-coat brigade in my time has been Alec Skelding, who thirty years ago or more was a 'quickie' bowler for Leicestershire. He always wears large white boots, reminding me of umpires at home, and he generally carries a flask of something which, he maintains, 'keeps out the cold and helps me to see straighter.' One day when Neil Harvey threw down the wicket with a brilliant return, it was touch and go whether the batsman had made his ground. In that husky sergeant-major parade-ground bark that every man who has played first-class cricket in England in recent times knows, Skelding called out: 'It's a photo finish but we can't wait for the photo, so he's not out.'

*

Many years ago, I came across two great characters in the very full world of umpiring: Tom Seamark and Bill Sutler. I found them when I was about twelve; they were the invention of Siegfried Sassoon — well, *almost* an invention. Seamark and Sutler were based on village umpires from Sassoon's boyhood, in Kent. Sassoon was born near Paddock Wood in 1886. Seamark and Sutler, therefore, were probably standing as umpires during the 1890s and early 1900s.

For those who have never met them, the two men appear briefly in Sassoon's *Memoirs of a Fox-Hunting Man*, a partly autobiographical book published in 1928. The cricket interlude comes when young George Sherston (Sassoon) is home from school to find that he is to play for his village, Butley, against the great rival side, Rotherden.

The umpires in their long white coats have placed the bails on the stumps, each at his own end, and they are still satisfying themselves that the stumps are in the requisite state of exact uprightness. Tom Seamark, the Rotherden umpire, is a red-faced sporting publican who bulks as large as a lighthouse. As an umpire he has certain emphatic mannerisms. When appealed to he expresses a negative decision with a severe and stentorian 'NOT OOUT': but when adjudicating that the batsman is out, he silently shoots his right arm towards the sky — an impressive and irrevocable gesture which effectively quells all adverse criticism. He is, of course, a tremendous judge of the game, and when not absorbed by his grave responsibilities he is one of the most jovial men you could meet with.

Bill Sutler, our umpire, is totally different. To begin with, he has a wooden leg. Nobody knows how he lost it; he does nothing to deny the local tradition that he was once a

70

soldier, but even in his cups he has never been heard to claim that he gave the limb for Queen and Country. It is, however, certain that he is now a cobbler (with a heavily waxed moustache) and a grossly partisan umpire. In direct contrast to Tom Seamark he invariably signifies 'Not out' by a sour shake of the head; when the answer is an affirmative one he bawls 'Hout' as if he'd been stung by a wasp. It is reputed that (after giving the enemy's last man out leg-before in a closely-fought finish) he was once heard to add, in an exultant undertone: 'And I've won my five bob.' He has also been accused of making holes in the pitch with his wooden leg in order to facilitate the efforts of the Butley bowlers.

Many village cricketers would today recognise Messrs Sutler and Seamark, even though Sassoon's match was played around 1903, perhaps just before. The game gets under way and brings us all the excitement of a close encounter and some lovely cameos of character sketches. Take the moment when the parson — who obviously fancies himself as something of a batsman — gets cleaned bowled without scoring.

The clock struck three, and the Reverend Yalden's leg-stump had just been knocked out of the ground by a vicious yorker from Frank Peckham. 'Hundred and seventeen. Five. Nought,' shouted the Butley scorer, popping his head out of the little flat-roofed shanty which was known as 'the pavilion'. The battered tin number-plates were rattled on to their nails on the scoring board by a zealous young hobbledehoy who had undertaken the job for the day.
'*Wodger* say last man made?' he bawled, though the scorer was only a few feet away from him.
'Last man, *Blob*,'
The parson was unbuckling his pads on a bench near by, and I was close enough to observe the unevangelical expression on his face as he looked up from under the brim of his panama hat with the M.C.C. ribbon round it. Mr Yalden was not a popular character on the Butley ground, and the hobbledehoy had made the most of a heaven-sent opportunity.

71

The Parson also kept wicket for the Rotherden side and he appears in the match once more. Sassoon obviously felt that Mr Yalden should continue to be seen as a less than charitable figure. It is the end of the game, almost, and Sassoon, or George Sherston as he is in the book, is going into bat with much depending on him.

When I arrived the Reverend Yalden was dawdling up the pitch in his usual duck-footed progress when crossing from one wicket to the other.

'Well, young man, you've got to look lively this time,' he observed with intimidating jocosity. But there seemed to be a twinkle of encouragement in Seamark's light blue eyes as I established myself in his shadow.

Dixon played the first three balls carefully. The fourth he smote clean out of the ground. The hit was worth six, but 'three all round and four over' was an immemorial rule at Butley. Unfortunately, he tried to repeat the stroke, and the fifth ball shattered his stumps. In those days there were only five balls to an over.

Peter Baitup now rolled up with a wide grin on his fringed face, but it was no grinning moment for me at the bottom end when Sutler gave me 'middle-and-leg' and I confronted impending disaster from Crump with the sun in my eyes. The first ball (which I lost sight of) missed my wicket by a 'coat of varnish' and travelled swiftly to the boundary for two byes, leaving Mr Yalden with his huge gauntlets above his head in an attitude of aggrieved astonishment. The game was now a tie. Through some obscure psychological process my whole being now became clarified. I remembered Shrewsbury's century and became as bold as brass. There was the enormous auctioneer with the ball in his hand. And there I, calmly resolved to look lively and defeat his destructive aim. The ball hit my bat and trickled slowly up the pitch. 'Come on!' I shouted, and Peter came gallantly on. Crump was so taken by surprise that we were safe home before he'd picked up the ball. And that was the end of the Flower Show Match.

Sassoon builds a carefree picture of a young man, really still a lad,

72

being for one moment a hero. Later, much later, Sherston goes to the Great War and sees a conflict where heroes die. In one of his poems, Sassoon slipped in a reminder of those soft Edwardian, youthful days; it was written in 1917:

Dreamers

Soldiers are citizens of death's grey land,
Drawing no dividend from time's to-morrows.
In the great hour of destiny they stand,
Each with his feuds, and jealousies, and sorrows.
Soldiers are sworn to action; they must win
Some flaming, fatal climax with their lives.
Soldiers are dreamers; when the guns begin
they think of firelit homes, clean beds and wives.

I see them in foul dug-outs, gnawed by rats,
And in the ruined trenches, lashed with rain,
Dreaming of things they did with balls and bats,
And mocked by hopeless longing to regain
Bank-holidays, and picture shows, and spats,
And going to the office in the train.

CHAPTER EIGHT

Civilization under the Sun

And now to Alfred Cochrane, writing in the second half of the nineteenth century. But he writes not of splendid days at Lord's or Taunton, but of something closer to us all; that one brief moment long forgotten by everyone except us. In 'big cricket' you have to be a batsman, a bowler or a wicket keeper. In proper cricket, that is in cricket kept in sight of chestnut and church spire, keenness is sometimes sufficient talent to get you into the side.

Once in the team, it is possible for even the most indifferent player to stay in. Somebody has to be number eleven, somebody has to make sure that the scoreboard is put away and that the square is roped off. Somebody has to take the blame for not stopping a four (off a bad ball of course), somebody has to take the good natured ribbing of the older members and shrug off the sometimes cruel asides of the youngsters.

But then, one afternoon, there is a moment of glory. It could be nothing more than not getting out while the skipper carefully grafts for the winning runs. And it may be, if you are fortunate, a catch. Even better, The Catch.

There is something special about a catch. Even the easy one which drops like a slowly lobbed beach ball may stop the heart. The memory of a fast, sharp, chance that goes to hand may last longer than the sweetest leg glance — at least for the player for whom it went to hand. Here then is Alfred Cochrane's description of The Catch, which holds good today as it did then:

The Catch
by
Alfred Cochrane

Stupendous scores he never made,
But perished ever with despatch;
No bowling genius he displayed,
But once, in a forgotten match,
    He made a catch.

No doubt a timely stroke of luck
Assisted him to do the trick;
He was at cover, and it stuck:
It travelled fairly low and quick —
    The kind that stick.

His friends the proud achievement classed
As fortune's most eccentric whim,
And ere a week or two had passed
The memory of the catch grew dim
    To all but him.

To all but him, for he relates,
With varying ornament and phrase,
The story to the man who waits
Unwilling in Pavilion ways,
    On rainy days.

The catch has grown in splendour now —
He had a dozen yards to run;
It won the match, as all allow,
And in his eyes there blazed the sun,
    And how it spun.

Life of old memories is compact,
And happy he for whom with speed
Blossoms a gorgeous tree, where fact
Has planted, in his hour of need,
    A mustard seed.

   For me, 'The Catch', is about village cricket, the heart of The
Game. It manages, certainly in Sussex and Kent, to survive in an
atmosphere not so far removed from that of forty or fifty years

ago, or indeed more. Here is Mary Russell Mitford writing more than 150 years ago:

I doubt if there be any scene in the world more animating or delightful than a cricket-match — I do not mean a set match at Lord's Ground, for money, hard money, between a certain number of gentlemen and players, as they are called — people who make a trade of that noble sport, and degrade it into an affair of bettings, and hedgings and cheatings, it may be, like boxing or horse-racing; nor do I mean a pretty fête in a gentleman's park, where one club of cricketing dandies encounter another such club, and where they show off in a graceful costume to a gay marquee of admiring belles, who condescend so to purchase admiration, and while away a long summer morning in partaking cold collations, conversing occasionally, and seeming to understand the game — the whole being conducted according to ball-room etiquette, so as to be exceedingly elegant and exceedingly dull. No! the cricket that I mean is a real solid old-fashioned match between neighbouring parishes, where each attacks the other for honour and a supper, glory and half-a-crown a man. If there be any gentlemen amongst them, it is well — if not, it is so much the better. Your gentleman cricketer is in general rather an anomalous character. Elderly gentlemen are obviously good for nothing; and your beaux are, for the most part, hampered and trammelled by dress and habit; the stiff cravat, the pinched-in-waist, the dandy-walk — oh! they will never do for cricket! Now, our country lads, accustomed to the flail or the hammer (your blacksmiths are capital hitters) have the free use of their arms; they know how to move their shoulders; and they can move their feet too — they can run; then they are so much better made, so much more athletic, and yet so much lissomer — to use a Hampshire phrase, which deserves at least to be good English. Here and there, indeed, one meets with an old Etonian, who retains his boyish love for that game which formed so considerable a branch of his education; some even preserve their boyish proficiency, but in general it wears away like the Greek, quite as certainly, and almost as fast; a few years of Oxford, or Cambridge, or the Continent, are sufficient to annihilate both the power and the inclination. No! a village match is the thing — where our highest officer — our conductor (to borrow a musical term) is but a little farmer's second son; where the spectators consist of the retired cricketers, the veterans of the green, the careful mothers, the girls, and all the boys of two parishes, together with a few amateurs, little above them in rank, and not at all in pretension; where laughing and shouting, and the very ecstasy of merriment and good-humour prevail: such a match, in short, as I attended yesterday, at the expense of getting twice wet through, and as I would attend tomorrow, at the certainty of having that ducking doubled.

A County Cricket Match, from *Our Village*,
Mary Russell Mitford

Some of the most engaging cricket passages have come from Hugh de Selincourt. He was born in 1878, just four years before English cricket died at the Oval to produce The Ashes. His *The Cricket Match*, is perhaps the most blissful portrayal of village cricket life. It was given to me to read by an English master for whom The Game meant more than anything. I carried that copy with me all over the world until it was 'lost' in Colombo. That was in 1959. Bemoaning my loss to a friend in what was then the capital of Ceylon, I was 'given on loan' to take back to England 'because it was rotting with the damp' a copy of the 1937 Times book to commemorate 150 years of the M.C.C. There towards the back was this gem from de Selincourt on village cricket:

The meeting of our cricket club in the library of the village hall bore ample witness to this spirit of derring-do. In Coronation Year — not to have a new coat of paint on the Pavilion! Absurd. Not to have water laid on — preposterous, in Coronation Year! And a small pipe extended to the square (at such trifling cost) so that in the event of a drought (we heard the perpetual rain falling outside and stamped in furious applause) — in the event of a drought (I repeat the word as the dauntless speaker repeated it) the pitch might be watered, the grass kept green, the turf in smiling, proper condition. There never was such a meeting. When enthusiasm simmered down a little from boiling point to more normal procedure the flame was turned up, relit as from fresh jets, by astute reference to his late Majesty's Playing Fields Fund, and to the 150th anniversary celebration of the great home of all cricket — 'Our own ground, gentlemen, being hardly less ancient; famed in story, though not named in *Wisden.*'

There never was such a meeting. It was almost funny. It was almost frightening. The staider members were thankful that the whole meeting did not emerge *en bloc* to the ground, collecting cans of petrol on their jubilant way, apply a match to the tumbledown wooden shack that disgraced the name of pavilion, and, while they watched the glad blaze in the dark, damp Spring night, vote vociferously that a new pavilion should arise in stone glory like a Phoenix from the smouldering ashes of the old.

On the Village Green, Hugh de Selincourt

Hugh de Selincourt would have been nearing sixty when he wrote that piece. He had played village cricket since he was fourteen. At his public school he had learned to play 'correctly'. He'd been coached in footwork, when to drop the wrists, how to get in line. In the village he learned how to laugh when his team mates laughed at him with his proper ways. As he said, 'The correct public schoolboy — myself — who turned out, rather shy and stiff, possibly, became as shy stiffness melted, the object of much witty good-humoured comment.'

His memory of the long-dead village warrior, Bill Awker, tells all. (The 'him' in the opening sentence is de Selincourt.)

Bill Awker, a wiry old chap who opened the bowling for a neighbouring village, found him especially amusing. Bill scorned to be dressed up in pretties. He lurched out in huge hob-nailed boots and corduroys to the wicket, took off his collar and tie, put them in the pocket of his jacket, which he removed and handed to the umpire. Then he rolled up his sleeves, fitted his cutty behind his buckled belt, spat on his hands, took the ball from his trouser pocket, stepped two paces back, and crying out 'Look out for this one, then,' proceeded to deal the swiftest lob that skimmed like a frantic little wood gone crazy over the grassy pitch at a petrifying pace, a real authentic daisy-cutter, dead on the wicket. Bill gave his hands an extra rub when he observed my exquisitely accoutred approach to the wicket, and greeted my immediate discomfiture with a horrid shout of laughter. Out came his cutty, out came exuberant puffs. I could never play him then. I am sure I could not play him now. Well, Old Bill has gone — rest his soul! — and many like him. I have not seen such bowling of late years (fortunately for my self-respect), and it is the man or boy not in full cricketing kit who is apt to rouse good-humoured comment now.

In Mary Russell Mitford's village cricket, good humour prevailed. Gerald Bullett's 'Village Cricket' goes one step further, for him it is 'civilization under the sun'.

Village Cricket
by
Gerald Bullett

Flowing together by devious channels
From farm and brickyard, forest and dene,
Thirteen men in glittering flannels
Move to their stations out on the green.

Long-limbed Waggoner, stern, unbudging,
Stands like a rock behind the bails.
Dairyman umpire, gravely judging,
Spares no thought for his milking pails.

Bricklayer bowls, a perfect length.
Grocery snicks and sneaks a run.
Law, swiping with all his strength,
Is caught by Chemist at mid-on.

Two to the boundary, a four and a six,
Put the spectators in fear of their lives:
Shepherd the slogger is up to his tricks,
Blithely unwary of weans and wives.

Lord of the manor makes thirty-four.
Parson contributes, smooth and trim,
A cautious twelve to the mounting score:
Leg-before wicket disposes of him.

Patient, dramatic, serious, genial,
From over to over the game goes on,
Weaving a pattern of hardy perennial
Civilization under the sun.

*

An attempt to recapture village cricket past was made in the late 1920s, appropriately at Hambledon. The occasion was recorded by one of the captains, Sir John Squire:

With a spontaneous effort the past can be partly recovered. Broadhalfpenny is now deserted; a bleak upland with a glorious view and Nyren's 'Bat and Ball' inn visited by an occasional slumbrous carter. Now and then it wakes up: a team, for old times' sake, feels like playing there. *Et Ego in Arcadia*. Eight years ago, on New Year's Day, certain Hambledonians (in the old Hambledon tradition, they roped in people from all over the county) raised an eleven to play against an eleven raised by me, as a protest against the way in which professional football was nibbling at the cricket season at both ends. The match was 'Hampshire Eskimos' versus 'Invalids' — the Eskimos subsequently turned themselves into a touring club, and long may they flourish, with their snow-white caps and blazers adorned by a running red fox.

The old spirit was recovered. The captain of the other side, Mr. Whalley-Tooker, had been in the Eton eleven the year I was born. The Master of the local hounds (Major Talbot-Ponsonby) gallantly produced a bye-day for his Hunt. Though intentional publicity there had been none several thousands of people turned out, charabancs from Portsmouth, two brass bands, and a vast concourse of riders. It is not surprising that the 'Bat and Ball' was soon at the end of its resources.

There was a matting wicket and we had arranged that we should play even were there a snowstorm, a deluge, or a fog. We were lucky; there was brilliant sunshine, and a cloudless blue sky, and, just as the game began, hounds found (we

80

were assured it wasn't a bagman) in roots, in the westward valley, and careered after him, in full sight of us, for several minutes. Some excellent cricket was played, among those distinguishing themselves on the winning side (the visitors won by eleven runs) being Mr. A. D. Peters (whose innings was worthy of Lord's), Mr. Howard Marshall, who had risen from a sick-bed in the expressed hope of hitting a six on Broadhalfpenny on New Year's Day, and actually hit the only six (through the inn window), and Mr. (now Sir) Walter Monckton, K.C., who was in his old form behind the stumps.

The evening ended at the 'George' in the old Hambledonian way: a large assembly, supper, flowing bowls, song, and even 'The Lost Chord' on a cornet. Some suggested making it an annual event. Had we had foul weather we might have tried next year. But a repetition of that perfect day, fox and all, was too much to expect; and it was wiser to let it remain a memory undimmed by an anti-climax.

The Cradle of Cricket, Sir John Squire M.C.C.

I wonder why village cricket appears to produce more good natured humour than almost any other sport. Certainly cricket writers achieve a high degree of humour — perhaps it is something about the remarkable antics necessary to bring together the apparently simple tasks of bowling a relatively small object towards a relatively well equipped batsman in order to get him out, so that others may come in to be got out. And what is the funniest piece of writing to illustrate this nonsense? Probably A. G. MacDonell captured it in 'England, Their England'. I had thought that everybody had read the famous cricket scene. But no. In compiling this manuscript I was surprised by the number of people who said, 'Oh yes, I know it, but I haven't actually read it.' I was even more pleased by the numbers who fell about laughing when I showed it to them. Here then is MacDonell's cricket match. The feared blacksmith, doing his Truman act (a few years earlier of course) is confident of an easy wicket:

He halted at the wicket before going back for his run, glared at Mr. Harcourt, who had been driven out to umpire by his colleagues — greatly to the regret of Mr. Bason, the landlord of the Shoes — glared at Mr. Southcott, took another reef in his belt, shook out another inch in his braces, spat on his hand, swung his arm three or four times in a meditative sort of way, grasped the ball tightly in his colossal palm, and then turned smartly about and marched off like a Pomeranian grenadier and vanished over the brow of the hill. Mr. Southcott, during these proceedings, leant elegantly upon his bat and admired the view. At last, after a long stillness, the ground shook, the grasses waved violently, small birds arose with shrill clamours, a loud puffing sound alarmed the butterflies, and the blacksmith, looking more like Venus Anadyomene than ever, came thundering over the crest. The world held its breath. Among the spectators conversation was suddenly hushed. Even the urchins, understanding somehow that they were assisting at a crisis in affairs, were silent for a moment as the mighty figure swept up to the crease. It was the charge of Von Bredow's Dragoons at Gravelotte over again.

But alas for human ambitions! Mr. Harcourt, swaying slightly from leg to leg, had understood the menacing glare of the bowler, had marked the preparation for a titanic effort, and, for he was not a poet for nothing, knew exactly what was going on. Mr. Harcourt sober had a very pleasant sense of humour, but Mr. Harcourt rather drunk was a perfect demon of impishness. Sober, he occasionally resisted a temptation to try to be funny. Rather drunk, never. As the giant whirlwind of vulcanic energy rushed past him to the crease, Mr. Harcourt, quivering with excitement and internal laughter, and wobbling, uncertainly upon his pins, took a deep breath and bellowed, 'No ball!'

It was too late for the unfortunate bowler to stop himself. The ball flew out of his hand like a bullet and hit third-slip, who was not looking, full pitch on the knee-cap. With a yell of agony third-slip began hopping about like a stork until he tripped over a tussock of grass and fell on his face in a bed of nettles, from which he sprang up again with another drum-splitting yell. The blacksmith himself was flung forward by his own irresistible momentum, started out of his wits by Mr. Harcourt's bellow in his ear, and thrown off his balance by his desperate effort to prevent himself from delivering the ball, and the result was that his gigantic feet got mixed up among each other and he fell heavily in the centre of the wicket, knocking up a cloud of dust and dandelion-seed and twisting his ankle. Rooks by hundreds arose in protest from the vicarage cedars. The urchins howled like intoxicated banshees. The gaffers gaped. Mr. Southcott gazed modestly at the ground. Mr. Harcourt gazed at the heavens. Mr. Harcourt did not think the world had ever been or could ever be again, quite such a capital place, even though he had laughed internally so much that he had got hiccups . . .

. . . The only other incident in the innings was provided by an American journalist, by name Shakespeare Pollock, an intensely active, alert, on the spot young man. Mr. Pollock had been roped in at the last moment to make up the eleven and Mr. Hodge and Mr. Harcourt had spent quite a lot of time on the way down trying to teach him the fundamental principles of the game. Donald had listened attentively and had been surprised that they made no reference to the Team Spirit. He decided in the end that the reason must have been simply that everyone knows all about it already, and that it is therefore taken for granted.

Mr. Pollock stepped up to the wicket in the lively manner of his native mustang, refused to take guard, on the ground that he wouldn't know what to do with it when he had got it, and, striking the first ball he received towards square-leg, threw down his bat, and himself set off at a great rate in the direction of cover-point. There was a paralysed silence. The rustics on the bench rubbed their eyes. On the field no one moved. Mr. Pollock stopped suddenly, looked round, and broke into a genial laugh.

'Darn me —' he began, and then he pulled himself up and went on in refined English, 'Well, well! I thought I was playing baseball.' He smiled disarmingly round.

'Baseball is a kind of rounders, isn't it, sir?' said cover-point sympathetically.

Donald thought he had never seen an expression change so suddenly as Mr. Pollock's did at this harmless, and true, statement. A look of concentrated, ferocious venom obliterated the disarming smile. Cover-point, simple soul, noticed nothing, however, and Mr. Pollock walked back to the wicket in silence and was out next ball . . .

. . . The batsmen came in. The redoubtable Major Hawker, the fast bowler, thrust out his chin and prepared to bowl. In a quarter of an hour he had terrified seven batsmen, clean bowled six of them, and broken a stump. Eleven runs, six wickets, last man two.

After the fall of the sixth wicket there was a slight delay. The new batsman, the local rate collector, had arrived at the crease and was ready. But nothing happened. Suddenly the large publisher, who was acting as wicketkeeper, called out, 'Hi! Where's Hawker?'

The words galvanized Mr. Hodge into portentous activity.

'Quick!' he shouted. 'Hurry, run, for God's sake! Bob, George, Percy, to the Shoes!' and he set off at a sort of gallop towards the inn, followed at intervals by the rest of the side except the pretty youth in the blue jumper, who lay down; the wicketkeeper, who did not move; and Mr. Shakespeare Pollock, who had shot off the mark and was well ahead of the field.

But they were all too late, even Mr. Pollock. The gallant Major, admitted by Mr. Bason through the back door, had already lowered a quart and a half of mild and bitter, and his subsequent bowling was perfectly innocuous, consisting, as it did, mainly of slow, gentle full pitches to leg which the village baker and even, occasionally, the rate collector hit hard and high into the long grass. The score mounted steadily.

'England, Their England', A. G. MacDonell

*

I think that it was a housemaster who told me that cricket was a festival of companionship. He thought that the most enjoyable and relaxing holidays were those spent at Cricket Festivals, or Cricket Weeks. He allowed that not everybody shared this view and remembered the time when his wife had not been overjoyed by his romantic offer of celebrating their 25th Wedding Anniversary by attending Scarborough Cricket Week.

C. P. Hawkes, writing in 1937, recalled the origins of the Cricket Week.

By its nature and constituents a Cricket Week is an institution peculiarly English, for it connotes the very essence and quiddity of an English countryside in summer and the deep-rooted democratic devotion to a national game which eliminates all mere social and intellectual distinctions.

The Cricket Week probably has its origins in Kent, at Canterbury. It started in the 1840s and came about because of the enthusiasms of amateur actors. For sound commercial reasons, the idea was to have cricket by day, and theatre during the evening. The troupe was led by Spencer Ponsonby, his brother Frederick and Tom Taylor, three fine actors and handsome cricketers. C. P. Hawkes paints a glorious picture of that summer of 1842:

In the first week of August the company embarked at London Bridge in the Ramsgate steampacket and on arrival at the Thanet port drove thence by coach to Canterbury. There they were put up at the Fountain Inn . . . They played two three-day matches and performed each evening in the old Orange Street theatre; and as he sat between innings in the pavilion-marquee Tom Taylor wrote the first Epilogue.

The cricketers were known as the Old Stagers (O.S.) and through them came one of the most famous clubs in the history of cricket, I Zingari (I Z.).

The week was so well patronized that it was repeated triumphantly each year until 1845, when a not unforeseen dilemma presented itself. The number available of good cricketers who could act and good actors who were competent cricketers was limited, and it was not uncommon for some of those needed at rehearsal to have to send substitutes up to the ground. There was a cross-pull, in fact, between field and footlights. A meeting accordingly was called at the old Blenheim Hotel in Bond Street early that

year, as the result of which the famous brotherhood of
I Zingari sprang into life, full-fledged like Pallas from the
head of Jove. This was to represent the purely cricketing
element, though all its officers and committee, with one
exception, were members of the original combination.

CHAPTER NINE

How to Beat the Aussies

In 1933 Hugh de Selincourt published *The Game of the Season*. As a portrait of southern agricultural cricketers and the well-bred skipper it is superb. It mirrors every schoolboy's dream of a mighty innings, and in one section does even better: it shows how to beat the Australians. Here are two cameos from the must-be-read book. The first is a marvellous sentence describing the toss between the Australian captain Armstrong (it would therefore have been 1921), and the Tillingfold captain:

> Mr Armstrong, as always, tossed with great skill, and showed no surprise at winning . . .

It reminded me of the old Sussex village cricketer, 'Pondweed' Philcox, now sadly in the winter of his years, who confessed to never having been surprised at *losing* a toss — nor sorry, because he would not have known what to do.

Having known exactly what to do, the Australians batted, but were all out for 39! Teddie White came in to bat for Tillingfold and faced a tight field, which, as everyone should know, has never bothered the true agriculturalist armed with a hefty bat:

> Teddie White did not go for niceties; he didn't bother about the field; it didn't matter to him where they happened to be placed; his one aim in batting was to put the ball out of their reach, out of the ground, much the safest place. But he had a kind heart, and noticing that the fieldsmen were crowded rather nearer to him than they usually were, as Mr Armstrong bowled, he cried out: 'Look out for yourselves then' as he might have done to careless boys at the village net, and lashed it for four.

There was a roar of applause. But Teddy White was not pleased. It was an ass of a shot — all along the ground — he had not properly got hold of it at all — you could never hit a six like that, the only really safe shot . . .

And here is, from another page of *The Game of the Season*, a reminder that in spite of the guile of the cleverest bowler, a man with a good shot is unforgiving to the bad ball:

It is difficult for any bowler to realize that a man can have one shot and one only like a mechanical toy. Down came the good-length ball on the middle stump — hit the swinging bat, flew between the fieldsmen — struck the wall.

With passages like that, how could the Australians have believed they were going to win? In real life, Australian sides have few off seasons. Here is a telling description of the Australians from one well qualified to know, Len Hutton, writing in *Just My Story*, published in 1956:

I admire the Australians' approach to the game; they have the utmost ability for producing that little extra, or instilling into the opposition an inferiority complex that can have, and has had, a crushing effect. Australians have no inhibitions.

And John Arlott, in his autobiography, *An Eye for Cricket*, published in 1979, endorsed this:

The Australians, throughout cricket history, have been quick to strike back even from a position of apparently imminent defeat.

The most famous occasion of striking back by the Australians occurred more than a hundred years ago, in 1882. The scene was Australia v. England at the Oval, August 28th, and 29th. It was, too, a reminder that the venerable W. G. Grace was far from invincible. Grace was captain of the England side. He took four catches and was top scorer with 4 in the first innings and 32 in the second.

In the first innings, the Australians got 63, England 101. Down came the rain and in the second innings the Australians made 122. In their second innings, however, England were all out for 77 and Australia had won. In the *Sporting Times* there followed a notice of deep mourning for English cricket:

> In Affectionate Remembrance
> of
> ENGLISH CRICKET
> which died at The Oval
> on
> 29th August, 1882
> Deeply lamented by a large circle of
> Sorrowing Friends and Acquaintances
> R.I.P.
> N.B. – The body will be cremated and
> the Ashes taken to Australia

Later that year, when the England side went to Australia, the English side managed to win and in Melbourne, the captain Lord Darnley, was given an urn containing ashes. He kept the trophy but it was passed to the M.C.C. when he died and has remained in the pavilion at Lord's ever since.

The Australians are renowned for their humour. The South African writer Louis Duffus toured with his country's side on many occasions and kept a record of his side's reactions to life outside South Africa in *Cricketers of the Veld*. One recollection concerned the sadly short lived N. A. Quinn, who died in 1934: Quinn had done well on the tour but had received his share of barracking. As Duffus remembered it, Quinn was getting fed up with the public side of being a tourist. Bowling at Bradman was one thing, facing autograph hunters, another. Irritated by the persistency of young collectors, Quinn was reluctant to sign when yet another presented his book and pencil with the customary, 'Give me your autograph, mister.' Dressed in suit and hat, and trying to conceal his identity, Quinn, who had been probably the most effective bowler on the tour, particularly against Bradman, replied 'I'm not a cricketer, son.'

'I know that, Mr Quinn,' said the youngster, 'but I'd like your signature all the same.'

Duffus also had an amusing story about 'Patsy' Hendren, which he claimed was set in Australia . . .

One day he was in a railway carriage in Australia when the train stopped and a young fellow entered his compartment. He wore white flannels and cricket boots but over his clothes a heavy overcoat buttoned up to his neck. He really looked like death. After a while 'Patsy' could not help commiserating with his fellow traveller, he looked so ill.

'You don't look too fit, ol' man,' he said. 'Is there anything I can do?'

The stranger replied in a husky whisper: 'I've been playing cricket and I dropped the star batsman when he had scored 99 runs.' He muffled up his throat in misery.

'Oh, that's bad,' said 'Patsy', glad to learn that his complaint was nothing more than a dropped catch, 'but it's all in the game.'

PLAYER'S CIGARETTES

S.A.C.A.

D. G. BRADMAN

'That wasn't all,' the sickly fellow went on softly, 'I dropped him again when he had 199.'

'Good heavens!' exclaimed Hendren, 'that *is* bad. If I'd done that I'd have cut my throat.'

In a faint whisper came the retort: 'That's just what I *have* done.'

1878, and F. R. Spofforth bowling for the Australians against C. I. Thornton's XI. 'Buns' Thornton was a great hitter of the ball and established his reputation during the late 1860s playing for Eton. This illustration of Spofforth is from the first ever Australian tour of England. That some in England didn't quite know what to expect is recalled by A. G. Steel writing in the Cricket *edition of the Badminton sports series. Steel was sitting with Spofforth watching from the Lord's Pavilion. The Reverend Arthur Ward is said to have remarked to Steel, 'I hear you are going to play against the niggers on Monday.' During that tour 'the niggers' lost only seven of their 37 matches.*

91

CHAPTER TEN

Three Protestant Ducks

Humour does not have to raise a laugh, a wry smile may often do — witness the following paragraph from the Westminster School Cricket Ledger of July, 1818:

> A challenge was also sent to us by the Charterhouse to play them at cricket, which was very properly refused, not only on account of their being such inferior players, but because it was thought beneath Westminster to accept a challenge from a private school.

Of a totally different style of humour is the following tale from Leicester. During a game against Sussex at Grace Road, a Sussex supporter having travelled all the way from the south coast, arrived early and reserved his seat by placing his anorak on it. He then went off in search of a score card. He came back to find his anorak on the rail and a beefy Leicester man on the seat.

'That's mine,' said the innocent southerner. 'I left my anorak on it.'

Without a smile came the reply, 'Sorry lad, up here it's backsides what bags seats, not anoraks.'

(Leicestershire lost, by the way.)

Very funny men are often very funny on any subject. When they are able to record that special wit, they are exceptional men. Arthur Marshall is an exceptionally funny man on cricket at his school in the 1920s. This is from *Girls Will Be Girls*:

> It always seemed to me, as a school boy reluctantly playing cricket in the 1920s, that a straight bat, so highly prized by the experts, was in my case mere foolishness, sending the ball, when I managed to make contact with it, feebly back

whence it had come. With a crooked bat there was at least a chance of deflecting the offensive weapon either to right or left and scoring a 'run'. To attempt to score anything at all may savour of self advertisement but that was never my aim. My sights were not set on a ribboned coat or a captain's hand on my shoulder smote. The sole purpose of a run was to remove me, however briefly, from the end where the action was . . .

The boys in the First and Second XIs, fully sighted and well able to protect themselves, were provided with a contraption called a 'box', a snug and reinforced padded leather compartment worn about the crutch and into which they tucked, I assume, what came easy to hand. It would have been considered a gross impertinence for any lesser player to plead for this protection. In the lower echelons, our genitals were expendable.

*

In 1981, a group of diplomats and journalists formed a knock-about side in the capital of the Soviet Union. Using a bat made by the then Moscow correspondent of the *Daily Telegraph*, Nigel Wade, they became known as the M.C.C. (or Moscow Cricket Club). A Russian stooge of the K.G.B. (he said it stood for Kiev Gas Board) asked one of their number what was going on. With a straight face, he was told that every time the ball was hit over the wall into the compound of a certain foreign legation, the ball was returned with a message inside. Oddly, the next time they played and the ball went over the wall, it failed to be returned.

*

The vision of the English parson sits easily in any picture of a soft summer, with chestnut tree, pretty pavilion, cool lemonade jug with thin muslin cover and the warm wood of the scorer's bench. Outdated Yesteryear? The 1930s? Then try this advertisement in *The Church Times* of 30 June 1967.

Old-fashioned Vicar (Tractarian) seeks colleague. Left-hand fast bowler preferred. Good golf handicap an asset but not essential. Fine Church with good music tradition. Parish residential and farming. Box H.V. 521.

In view of this, perhaps the remarks of Richard Lloyd, the organist at Durham Cathedral, in a letter to *The Times* in 1985 are not so surprising:

When Dr. Cyril Alington was Dean of Durham, he was sometimes asked to preach at other cathedrals. On his own admission, his thoughts as he processed up the nave were not on things heavenly, nor even on the architecture, but on whether the nave would take spin.

(The nave at Durham, from memory, is not remarkably true. However, the croquet lawn nearby, is another matter.)

The complete image of the parson at play or the Dean wondering about spin at Durham is to be found in this poem by Norman Gale:

The Church Cricketant
by
Norman Gale

> I bowled three sanctified souls
>   With three consecutive balls!
> What do I care if Blondin trod
>   Over Niagara falls?
> What do I care for the loon in the Pit
>   Or the gilded Earl in the Stalls?
> I bowled three curates once
>   With three consecutive balls!
>
> I caused three Protestant 'ducks'
>   With three consecutive balls!
> Poets may rave of lily girls
>   Dancing in marble halls!
> What do I care for a bevy of yachts
>   Or a dozen or so of yawls?
> I bowled three curates once
>   With three consecutive balls!

I bowled three cricketing priests
　With three consecutive balls!
What if a critic pounds a book
　What if an author squalls?
What do I care if sciatica comes,
　Elephantiasis calls?
I bowled three curates once
　With three consecutive balls!

But just to show that some men of the cloth don't have a sense of humour:

Churchwardens' Presentments, Archdeaconry of Chichester, 1622

I present Raphe West Edward Hartley Richard Slaughter William Martin Richard Martin Junior together with others in theire company whose names I have noe notice of for playing at Crecket in the Churchyeard on Sunday the fifte of May after sufficient warning given to the Contrary for three speciall reasons. First for that it is Contrary to the 7th article. Secondly for that they use to breake the Chirchwindowes with the ball and thirdly for that a litle childe had like to had her braynes beaten out with a Cricket batt. And also I present Richard Martin senior & Thomas West the old Churchwardens for defending and mayntayning them in it.

*

Cricket has also had its more macabre moments. In 1848, a Mr Ingersoll of Lewisham, which was not far from the Greenwich Naval Hospital, put together an almost grotesque match. He set up a game between a team of one-legged sailors to play one-armed sailors. Furthermore, it was a two-day game. This is the match report carried in the *London Illustrated News* of Saturday, 9 September 1848, together with an equally grotesque illustration of the event:

By the kind permission of the authorities of Greenwich

Hospital, the hardy veterans of that splendid establishment were entertained at a cricket match on Monday and Tuesday, in the Priory grounds, near Lewisham. The novelty of the conditions upon which alone these worn-out sons of the ocean would be allowed to enter the lists, was the cause of a large and fashionable party attending each day. These conditions were, that twenty-two men should be chosen for the field, one half of whom should be minus an arm, and the other a leg! Yet there was no lack of candidates for the honours of the bat and ball, and the number was very soon selected. The weather, too, was beautifully fine; the locality selected for the display a most charming spot; and the spectators as well as the actors appeared to be highly amused.

A large tent had been erected on the southern side of the field, and within it was spread forth an ample supply of the creature comforts of this life, to which the dilapidated tars did ample justice. They were invited to this entertainment by Mr. Ingersoll, of Lewisham, who, in conjunction with Mr. Ireland and Mr. Staunton, had got it up at their sole expense, in addition to distributing a sum of money amongst the competitors. Upon the first day the wickets were pitched, and the sports commenced shortly after two o'clock, the bands striking up 'Rule Britannia', the eleven one-armed men taking the first innings; and during the whole time the bats and balls were at work, the spectators were kept in an almost continuous roar of laughter by the grotesque figures the poor old veterans made as they measured their length on the slippery sward in their vain efforts to reach the ball, or to exercise their diminished 'under-standing' beyond their ordinary gait to reach the goal in time.

Upon the first day the one-arms made 50 runs in the first start, and 41 at the second. On Tuesday they assembled again with renewed vigour; and now the wooden legs went at it in high glee. Their first innings made 32, and their second 43; thus leaving the game to the one-arms by 16. Nothing could exceed the delight with which they appeared to enjoy the sport, or the kindness and courteous attention of Mr. Ingersoll to all their wants. The game was concluded by six o'clock; and then the hardy old blue-coats marched in procession from the ground, headed by the band, banners, etc., and were again entertained at a party feast by Mr. Ingersoll, at the Black Bull Inn.

CHAPTER ELEVEN

Close of Play

Perhaps it is too easy to dwell on the origins of The Game, but those origins certainly seem to have had something often lacking in today's game. It would be wrong to suggest that times past were better times; there are heaps of examples where The Game was in disgrace, even with its most devoted admirers. Let me, however, offer a view from the 1986 winter tour of the West Indies. Simon Barnes writing in *The Times* put the modern game of Test cricket in some certain perspective:

> What can be done to remove this curse from a once beautiful game? For surely Saturday showed us the unacceptable face of cricket. After the wonders of Sabina Park, Jamaica, where we had three days of good, clean, vicious fun, at the Queen's Park Oval in Trinidad we were forced to watch the ugly side of cricket — a full day of spin.
>
> Let us not mince words. The batsmen were being deliberately tormented. Edmonds and Emburey were unscrupulously using every vicious device in their devious repertoires to make the ball buzz and fizz and they made life impossible for the best batsmen in the world. They did so coldly and cynically; their cruel aim was to cause mental torture in the batsmen. And they succeeded.
>
> All the helmets and armour in the world were no protection against the evil-minded policies of England's shameful pair. Not even Richards was able utterly to defy this scourge of the modern game.
>
> Edmonds bowled longer and with less luck; Emburey had the luck instead, which was not fair because it was Edmonds's birthday.
>
> England played it sportingly for a while, cheerfully

throwing runs away with old-fashioned bouncers; but they resorted to the calculated torment of spin and briefly took control of the game. Had the English batsmen given them some runs to bowl at, the spin might have worked the miracle England sought.

But the question remains and cannot be ducked: what can be done to remove the curse of spin from the game? A white line threequarters of the way up the pitch, beyond which the ball must not bounce? A bar suspended at half-way, under which the ball must pass, to eliminate the unfair flighted ball? Perhaps the bowler should be limited to one ball that turns per over.

Surely no spin should be bowled to tail-enders. The umpire must step in. When a bowler turns the ball sideways and refuses to aim at the batsman surely the umpire must tell him to return at once to normal cricket and to try to knock the batsman's head off. What is cricket supposed to be about, after all?

Longing for things gone by is not new. In 1874 even, E. E. Bowen was rhyming and musing on players long since dead:

> There were splendid cricketers then, you know,
>   There were splendid cricketers then;
> The littlest drove for a mile or so,
>   And the tallest drove for ten;
> With Lang to bowl and Hankey to play,
>   Webbe and Walker to score and stay —
> And two that I know but may not say —
> But we are a pitiful race of clay,
>   And never will score again.
>   For all of we,
>   Whoever we be,
> Come short of the giants of old, you see.

One can say rather grandly that it is The Game that will survive all the wishes and prejudices of its closest fans. It is no longer an important aspect of the social scene as P. G. Wodehouse observed in *Piccadilly Jim*:

Oh, I am so glad you have begun to take an interest in cricket. It is simply a social necessity in England . . .

As a romantic I confess that of all the glorious words written about it, just two lines convey the spirit and feeling of contentment of an afternoon's cricket. Here then, two lines of Arlott:

> Dozing in deck-chair's gentle curve,
> Through half-closed eyes I watched the cricket . . .

But to close, this reflective epitaph of the season from G. D. Martineau, which in my mind I have seen time and again as I walked across chilled grass from a silent pavilion:

It is cold walking over the ground this evening.

Something that was full of warm life and expectation has gone out of the air, and has been replaced by chilly dullness, foreign to the summer season, painful to the subconscious mind.

The icy drops of that short storm had in them none of the tenderness that told merely of a drying wicket and a bowler's day on the morrow. Instead they whipped the pavilion roof with an unfriendly clatter, and the sky showed an unbroken grey to anxious watchers from near-by windows. Now the club flag has been hauled down, and the bare mast stands up like a desolate monument to the dying season.

A solitary match between two scratch elevens remains to be played on the ground, and the bowling screens accordingly, are left to flap a faint protest, with the last pink of the sunset blessing them.

Far out in the centre can be seen, dimly, the worn patches; scars on the turf, eloquent of bowlers' toil, soon to be hidden in the quick growing green. What a season!

So one reflects, going mentally through the tale of hard struggles and their accompanying feats of individual brilliance. It may be that there will be the memory of some personal success, which quickens the pulse and brings back a tingle to the blood. Glad, honest, youthful pride! That was a good day.

Again will come the feel of that late cut, the sublime shudder up the blade that told of an unanswerable boundary;

and again one lives the moment of that smart run out: the rash call, the cat-like spring, the lightening return, bails flying . . . a joyous dream that will come back through long years.

The rising wind sends a ripple over the outer grass, and the coldness of it drives one hurriedly down the path past the churchyard — for nearly the last time.

The western sky has turned jet-black, and pin-hole lights are flickering on the downs.

A wonderful year; it is right that it should die so beautifully.

K. S. Ranjitsinhji, Maharaja Jamsahib of Nawanagar — the great Ranji. An old friend saw him at Hove and remembered that it was the first time that he knew batting to be an art form. Ranji came to England and won his Blue at Cambridge in 1893. His was a dazzling career. He once played three games in one day and scored a century in each. Perhaps it was no wonder that Ranji — who chose to play for Sussex — was the first batsman to score more than 3000 runs in one season. His average during 12 seasons at Sussex was an enviable 63.24.

EPITAPH

As in life so in death a bat of renown,
Slain by a lorry (three ton);
His innings is over, his bat is laid down:
To the end a poor judge of a run.

George McWilliam

Bibliography

Alington, Cyril, *Edward Lyttelton*, John Murray, 1943
Arlott, John, *Jack Hobbs*, John Murray & Davis-Poynter, 1981
British Life and Thought, Longmans, 1941
Brodribb, Gerald (Comp.), *The English Game*, Hollis & Carter, 1948
Bryant, Sir Arthur, *The Age of Elegance*, Collins
Cardus, Neville, *Cricket*, Longmans, Green & Co. 1930
de Selincourt, Hugh, *The Cricket Match*, Rupert Hart-Davis, 1924
de Selincourt, Hugh, *The Game of the Season*, Rupert Hart-Davis, 1933
Duffus, Louis, *Cricketers of the Veld*, Sampson Low, Marston
England, An Anthology, Macmillan, 1944
Gale, Frederick, *The Game of Cricket*, 1888
Harris, Lord, *A Few Short Runs*, John Murray
Miller, Keith, *Cricket Crossfire*, Oldbourne, 1956
Nyren, John, *The Young Cricketer's Tutor*, 1873 (6th Edition)
Parker, Eric, *The History of Cricket*, Seeley Service
Pycroft, Rev. James, *The Cricket Field*, 1873
Pycroft, Rev. James, *Oxford Memories,* 1886
Sassoon, Siegfried, *Memoirs of a Fox-Hunting Man*, Faber & Faber, 1928
Sassoon, Siegfried, *The War Poems*, Faber & Faber, 1983
Strutt, J., *Sports and Pastimes of the Peoples of England*, 1876
Warner, Sir Pelham, *Lord's 1787-1945*, George C. Harrap, 1946
The Young Cricketer's Tutor, 1873 (6th Edition)